Praise for
Change to Strange

"It's not just a war for talent out there, it's a war for the right talent. Cable sheds light on how managers can identify and attract the right people to turn strategy into reality."

—Susan Ashford, Associate Dean for Leadership Programming and the Executive MBA Program, University of Michigan

"*Change to Strange* takes the mystery out of the gap between strategy and strategy execution. Daniel underscores that success is dependent on the quality of your workforce, specific targets, and disciplined measurement. The book provides a useful process and a set of questions that your leadership team needs to address to create a great organization that stands above competitors."

—Stan Kelly, Senior Vice President, Wachovia Corporation

"In an era of over-emphasis on best practices and benchmarking, it is so refreshing to see a blueprint for how an organization can invest in its people to truly drive competitive advantage and create uncommon value for its customers and owners. Daniel Cable's insightful, practical, and rigorous 'strange workforce value chain' will help your organization build a workforce with distinctive and compelling capabilities that better serve your customers and beat the competition."

—Christian M. Ellis, Senior Vice President, Sibson Consulting, A Division of Segal

"*Change to Strange* helps you ask the right questions about what will differentiate you in the marketplace and the strange (distinctive, extraordinary) steps you must take to make it happen. Be strange; get *Change to Strange* and have fun cooking up the special sauce your customers will love and your competition will find tough to imitate."

—Ben Schneider, Senior Research Fellow, VALTERA; Professor Emeritus, University of Maryland; and author of *Winning the Service Game*.

"Cable's model is highly thought-provoking. The book is full of great ideas for standing out from the competition and getting your workforce fully engaged!"

—Sara Rynes, Editor, Academy of Management Journal; Murray Professor of Management, University of Iowa

"What a great read! I found plenty of great ideas and examples in this book that I can use at VIF, and now my executive team is reading it."

—David B. Young, Chief Executive Officer, Visiting International Faculty Program

change to strange

W Wharton School Publishing

In the face of accelerating turbulence and change, business leaders and policy makers need new ways of thinking to sustain performance and growth.

Wharton School Publishing offers a trusted source for stimulating ideas from thought leaders who provide new mental models to address changes in strategy, management, and finance. We seek out authors from diverse disciplines with a profound understanding of change and its implications. We offer books and tools that help executives respond to the challenge of change.

Every book and management tool we publish meets quality standards set by The Wharton School of the University of Pennsylvania. Each title is reviewed by the Wharton School Publishing Editorial Board before being given Wharton's seal of approval. This ensures that Wharton publications are timely, relevant, important, conceptually sound or empirically based, and implementable.

To fit our readers' learning preferences, Wharton publications are available in multiple formats, including books, audio, and electronic.

To find out more about our books and management tools, visit us at whartonsp.com and Wharton's executive education site, exceed.wharton.upenn.edu.

change to strange

Create a Great Organization by
Building a Strange Workforce

Daniel M. Cable

Vice President, Publisher: Tim Moore
Wharton Editor: Yoram (Jerry) Wind
Acquisitions Editor: Jennifer Simon
Editorial Assistant: Pamela Boland
Development Editor: Russ Hall
Associate Editor-in-Chief and Director of Marketing: Amy Neidlinger
Publicist: Amy Fandrei
Marketing Coordinator: Megan Colvin
Cover Designer: John Barnett
Managing Editor: Gina Kanouse
Senior Project Editor: Kristy Hart
Copy Editor: Language Logistics LLC
Proofreader: Water Crest Publishing
Senior Indexer: Cheryl Lenser
Senior Compositor: Gloria Schurick
Manufacturing Buyer: Dan Uhrig

Wharton School Publishing

© 2007 by Pearson Education, Inc.
Publishing as Wharton School Publishing
Upper Saddle River, New Jersey 07458

Wharton School Publishing offers excellent discounts on this book when ordered in quantity for bulk purchases or special sales. For more information, please contact U.S. Corporate and Government Sales, 1-800-382-3419, corpsales@pearsontechgroup.com. For sales outside the U.S., please contact International Sales at international@pearsoned.com.

Printed in the United States of America

First Printing April, 2007

ISBN 0-13-157222-9

Pearson Education LTD.
Pearson Education Australia PTY, Limited.
Pearson Education Singapore, Pte. Ltd.
Pearson Education North Asia, Ltd.
Pearson Education Canada, Ltd.
Pearson Educatión de Mexico, S.A. de C.V.
Pearson Education—Japan
Pearson Education Malaysia, Pte. Ltd.

Library of Congress Cataloging-in-Publication Data

Cable, Dan.

  The change to strange : create a great organization by building a strange workforce / Daniel M. Cable.

    p. cm.

  ISBN 0-13-157222-9 (hardback : alk. paper) 1. Organizational effectiveness. I. Title.

HD58.9.C33 2007

658.3'01—dc22

                                                                    2006100415

To Alison

Contents

Acknowledgments

I've been told acknowledgments should be made to people without whom this book would not have been possible. That's why I first want to acknowledge my parents. Without them neither I nor this book would have been possible, and I thank you for always (well, usually) encouraging me to try new directions.

I also want to acknowledge all the executives and MBAs who have sat through my spiel in the form of a class or leadership session. You helped me make my ideas better and more useful, and now here they are in a book!

Tim Judge, thank you for encouraging me and teaching me stuff throughout my career. Can you keep doing that?

I thank Bob Emmerichs, who helped me apply the Workforce Value Chain to public and not-for-profit organizations, and also helped me work through some early outlines of this book.

I thank Mindy Storrie, formerly with General Electric's Durham Engine Facility, now Director of the Kenan-Flagler Leadership Initiative. Mindy taught me so much about linking a workforce's behaviors and obsessions with company strategy, and about the strange and wonderful competition machine that is the Durham Engine Facility.

Some individuals worked many hours with me trying to see how the Strange Workforce Value Chain applied to and informed their own organizations. I thank:

- Lynn Boggs and Diana Best with Novant Health

- VADM Gerry Hoewing, USN (ret) and Murray Rowe, SES (ret), Navy Manpower, Personnel, Training and Education Enterprise

- Stan Kelly with Wachovia

- Rear Admirals Jim McPherson, Bruce MacDonald, and Jim Houck with The Navy JAG Corps

- Roy Morrow with Lincoln Electric

- Scott Whalen with W.K. Dickson

Finally, I want to thank Jen Simon and Pearson for taking a chance on me.

About the Author

Daniel M. Cable is a Sarah Graham Kenan Distinguished Scholar and Professor of Management in the Kenan-Flagler Business School at the University of North Carolina. Dan's areas of research, teaching, and consulting include corporate culture, person-organization fit, performance management, the organizational entry process, selection systems, and total rewards. Dan received his PhD and Masters Degrees from Cornell University, and his BA from Pennsylvania State University. Dan received the McCormick Award for Distinguished Research Contributions from the Society for Industrial and Organizational Psychology.

Dan also likes to renovate old houses. He has renovated houses in Atlanta GA, Boone NC, Raleigh NC, and Chapel Hill NC.

Preface

To nail down a competitive advantage, your organization needs to do or create something distinctive that customers find valuable. In other words, you can't be great if you just do what everyone else does—you have to do something unique and out of the ordinary. If you want to stand out above your competitors, you can't just be "normal."

Nowadays, most organizations claim that their *people* are their competitive advantage. But most organizations build workforces that really are not very different from their competitors'. Most organizations, it turns out, treat their people just about the same as most other organizations. In fact, companies deliberately benchmark their people practices to the industry average. Not surprisingly, there is nothing particularly distinctive about most organizations' workforces and nothing the organization produces is particularly noteworthy from a customer standpoint—nothing very strange.

Put these together, and what situation do you have? You have organizations hoping to achieve extraordinary results with a solidly ordinary, normal workforce.

Pssst. Listen. I'll tell you a secret since you took the time to read this preface. If your competitive advantage depends on your people creating something valuable and distinctive, then your workforce can't be normal. To get your extraordinary results, you are going to have to build yourself a workforce that is extraordinary in a way that customers care about. To build a great organization, you need to build a strange workforce.

This book tells you why and how you should build your strange workforce. I present an approach called the *Strange Workforce Value Chain*, which is useful for two reasons:

- To develop your story about how your workforce is going to make customers want to give their money to you and not your competitors.

- To measure and manage the extent to which your workforce is helping make your extraordinary story come true.

So, read this book to get both the vision and the tools for building a strange workforce and getting your competitive advantage. Here is how to read and use this book:

- Read it the whole way through once. You'll see lots of suggested activities and meetings along the way—just read them, but don't try to do them the first time through. Make sure you don't skip the last chapter on measurement. The processes in this book place a heavy emphasis on measurement and metrics, so to engage in the activities you'll really need a process for measuring fuzzy concepts.

- Once you read the book one time, you can see which suggested activities are what you and your organization need. You can think about who in your organization will help you on the quest for a strange workforce. Then you can go back and re-read the needed sections again and start to make it happen in your organization.

Just in case you are reading this book while standing in an airport right now and you need to put down it down to run and catch your flight, here is the most basic logic you need to move forward:

Great organizations possess a
Sustained Competitive Advantage

They get it by creating and delivering something to the market that is
Valuable, Rare, and Hard to Imitate

Creating and delivering this value demands the disciplined obsession of a
Strange Workforce

And the way to build and focus a strange workforce is by using
Strategic Measurements and
Strange Workforce Architecture

Figure P.1 The basic logic of a strange workforce: Why you want one, how you get one.

1

Be Strange.
Be Very Strange.

Do you want to build a great organization? Then you need to build a strange workforce. Does the word "strange" next to your workforce bother you? Strange means "out of the ordinary; unusual or striking; differing from the normal."[1] Maybe having a strange workforce sounds a little risky to you—being different from normal doesn't sound comfortable and doesn't sound like you'd fit in. But when it comes to winning customers

> **Strange means "out of the ordinary; unusual or striking; differing from the normal."[1]**

and beating down competition, you don't want to fit in. Success will not come from being like your competition. You need your organization to be out

---

[1] The American Heritage® Dictionary of the English Language, Fourth Edition.
Copyright © 2000 by Houghton Mifflin Company.

of the ordinary, unusual, and striking. If your workforce is how you beat the competition, then you can't build a great organization unless you build a strange workforce.

When customers interact with great organizations, they notice something different about their products, prices, or services that makes them say "Wow!" and tell other people about their experience. What do you think makes an organization's products, services, or prices noticeably different to customers? If your workforce creates or delivers the thing that your customers want, and your workforce is just about the same as your competitors', what exactly will customers notice about you? Nothing. What will make them excited about your organization? Nothing. Let's face it: You need your workforce to impress customers deeply and profoundly if you want to build a great organization.

> **Let's face it: You need your workforce to impress customers deeply and profoundly if you want to build a great organization.**

Welcome to the concept of the *strange workforce*. A strange workforce is what makes customers notice your organization and want to give you their money. This book will help you build a strange workforce that creates something customers notice and makes them say, "I want that."

Strange Mechanics

General Electric has a facility that builds airplane engines in Durham, North Carolina. The mechanics who assemble the engines are strange compared to the mechanics at other airplane engine facilities.

Durham Engine Facility mechanics are personally obsessed with on-time delivery, no defects, and no accidents. They work in teams that are in charge of their own schedules, budgets, and overtime and routinely rearrange their work schedules to hit delivery targets. They are willing and able to purchase new tools and invent new assembly processes that save time, reduce physical strain, and make defects less likely.

The mechanics rotate themselves into leadership roles responsible for attending business meetings where they report and learn financial, regulatory, and safety information and where they develop company policy (such as a reduction-in-force process). They report the information from these meetings back to their teams, which meet together for one hour every day.

All of the mechanics report directly to the plant manager; there is no middle management. The teams of mechanics personally perform the hiring, performance management, and discipline of their coworkers—if a mechanic is causing an engine to get behind schedule, he will hear about it from a peer in short order. Then if the one-on-one feedback doesn't change his behavior, the entire team gets involved to remedy the problem.

An intact team of Durham Engine Facility mechanics builds an airplane engine from scratch. They start by reading the blueprint and planning out the assembly procedure, and they end by reviewing the results of the engine test after it is shipped. This means that as a group of mechanics, the team needs to acquire the tools and parts, track material shortages, develop and modify schedules to meet ship date, plan shifts and overtime, ensure quality of parts and engine build, conduct the final inspection, ship to the test site, and conduct post-test fault review. Every mechanic on each team rotates into each of these roles and is able to assemble each part of each engine. Teams attach their business cards on their engines with pride as they go out the door.

Are these engine mechanics strange? Well, compare them to typical airplane mechanics. Mechanics in typical assembly plants are fairly narrow in the scope of their tasks, contribute skilled manual labor, and are judged based on their ability to perform one task very efficiently. Honestly, normal mechanics might not enjoy working at the Durham Engine Facility. An ordinary assembly person does not fit into a flexible clan of mechanics who obsess about ship dates and budgets, spend upwards of 12 hours hiring a single new mechanic to the team, discipline coworkers about slack behavior, attend management meetings to learn and teach better ways to do things, and communicate it back to their coworkers so that they can build product cheaper, better, and faster. Typical mechanics like to work fairly independently of others and do not feel comfortable building consensus, making business decisions as a group, or resolving daily interpersonal conflicts. Durham Engine Facility mechanics are a strange tribe.

What kind of business results does this strange, obsessed workforce create? In five years, this workforce reduced the cost of producing a CF6 engine by 10% each year, resulting in a 30% cost improvement on a twenty-year-old product.[2] This workforce reduced the average number of defects 75%, from four per engine to one per engine. They did not miss one on-time shipment in 38 months and 500 engines. They were close to producing twice the engines with the same number of employees. Do you think that Boeing, their largest customer, noticed 75% fewer defects and immaculate on-time delivery? Let's just say that the Durham Engine Facility did not lay off one person and remained profitable during the airline downturn from 2001 to 2003. Let's just say that if you are a producer of airplane engines, you are going to have a hard time beating the Durham Engine Facility. But it's not magic—it's just a strange workforce.

People as Competitive Advantage

Lots of companies claim that "people are our competitive advantage." It's funny when they make this claim because many of the people who lead those companies don't know what it means. In a classroom full of business leaders from different companies, most of them raise their hands when asked, "How many of you work for a company that says people are its competitive advantage?" But ask one of them what that really means at his or her company and you don't get a good answer. You often get that deer-in-the-headlights blank stare. Or you get what I call a B-minus answer that sounds like this:

> **"Well, our people *do* everything. When you call and order from us, who answers the phone? Our people. And who delivers the product? Our people. So, people *are* our organization. We are nothing without our people."**

But it's sort of fun to ask the question: Doesn't your competition also have people? People in competing companies answer the phone and deliver product, right? This is a little like saying that electricity is your competitive advantage. No doubt, it's really *useful* to have electricity. With it, you can use computers and lights. It would be hard to envision running your organization without electricity, but electricity does not give your organization a competitive advantage

---

[2] Fishman, C., "Engines of Democracy," *Fast Company*. October 1999, 175-202.

because your competitors have electricity too. So, sure, having employees do things is valuable, but that doesn't make them your competitive advantage.

It's also funny that many of the very leaders who claim that people are their competitive advantage put little personal energy into building their workforce. They hire people after 30-minute interviews based on gut feel about "fit." They race through performance evaluations to get them out of the way until next year so they can get back to their "real work." Their top HR folks are accountants who got saddled with payroll 23 years ago and stuck around long enough that they eventually were promoted to head of HR. Their VP of HR couldn't cut it in sales so he got sent to HR where he "couldn't do too much damage." As a result of these career inroads, the person in charge of your most important asset may not do much thinking about competitive advantage, and may not even know who your competition is. There may not be anyone in your company thinking about the ways your people need to be strange.

> **There may not be anyone in your company thinking about the ways your people need to be strange.**

How *Can* a Workforce Give an Organization a Competitive Advantage?

Three things: First, your workforce obviously must create something valuable to the marketplace—that is, there must be customers who want or need what your workforce does or creates, who are willing to pull dollars out of their wallets or budgets and give it to your company. However, if there is money to be made doing something, then other organizations are likely to do it too. Even if you are the first company to offer the desirable product or service, competitors will be drawn to the money like moths to light. Using a workforce to create something valuable simply represents the table stakes of being in business, not for beating down competition.

Second, your workforce also must create something rare, something unique that sets your organization apart. Your workforce needs to create some special sauce that makes customers say, "Sure I could get this from seven different companies, but this one does this certain thing that I like best, so I'm giving them my money." It might be the lowest price, the quickest delivery

> **Your workforce needs to create some special sauce that makes customers say, "Sure I could get this from seven different companies, but this one does this certain thing that I like best, so I'm giving them my money."**

time, or the comfort of talking to a person who remembers customers' names and what they usually order. It might be any number of things, but there needs to be something that differentiates your organization and adds special value in the minds of customers.

Third: If your organization's special sauce—the unique valuable thing that you offer—is easy for competitors to copy, then you don't have a sustained competitive advantage. Wal-Mart was an early initiator of some supply chain management practices that were quite valuable and rare. By partnering with suppliers and pushing much of the stock management onto them, Wal-Mart created value for customers. How? It was more likely that product would be in stock when consumers walked in the door. It allowed Wal-Mart to lower prices because they didn't need to pay as many people to manage the stock, and also because suppliers could offer cheaper prices to Wal-Mart when they had more lead time. The supply chain process gave Wal-Mart a competitive advantage, but only for a little while because other large retailers were able to copy Wal-Mart's practices. To develop and keep a competitive advantage over

> **For your workforce to be a sustained source of competitive advantage, your workforce needs to do something that is valuable and unique in customers' eyes and hard for competitors to imitate.**

a long period of time, you need to offer something valuable, rare, and hard to imitate—something that competitors can't see or maybe can't understand. Or perhaps even if they can see it and understand it, they are not willing or able to actually do it in a way that customers appreciate. For your workforce to be a sustained source of competitive advantage, your workforce needs to do something that is valuable and unique in customers' eyes and hard for competitors to imitate.

I call this a strange workforce: Definitely out of the ordinary and unexpected[3]; unusual or striking[4]; slightly odd or even a bit weird.[5] If you want to beat down competition and win, then you want to cultivate a strange workforce that is *obsessive*—intensely preoccupied with something. Obsessing means worrying about something unevenly, much more than other things and much more than other normal people who might be mildly concerned with that same thing. You want competitors to look at your workforce, shake their heads half in wonder and say, "We wouldn't be able to do that." Have you ever worked with someone brilliant who seemed to have a "strange genius," "unique gift," or "weird instinct" for creating results? You knew you could never keep up with them because they were so talented and so *obsessed* that they made the others look like they are just playing around. You want to create that same reaction in your competitors and customers, but with your workforce. Are you starting to get turned on to strange? You *want* to be strange.

Naturally, not just any type of strange obsession will win your customers' business. Your workforce needs to obsess on things that customers value but that other workforces—in particular, your competitors' workforces—do not obsess on. Obsessing, for example, about whether or not your rotors are going to arrive next week so that your airplane engine can be shipped to the customer on time (Durham Engine Facility). Or whether the new cell phone style is really as thin and sleek as physically possible (Motorola). Or about exercise and working out and toning the body every day with the right athletic equipment (Nike). Or providing open source software so that the world is not captive to Microsoft (Red Hat). Cultivating a strange workforce that obsesses about things that customers care about is a

> **Cultivating a strange workforce that obsesses about things that customers care about is a necessary condition if you are going to get a sustained competitive advantage through your workforce.**

[3] WordNet ® 2.0, © 2003 Princeton University.

[4] The American Heritage® Dictionary of the English Language, Fourth Edition. Copyright © 2000 by Houghton Mifflin Company.

[5] WordNet, ibid.

necessary condition if you are going to get a sustained competitive advantage through your workforce. What does your workforce obsess about? What *could* they obsess about?

Where Will I Get My Strange Workforce?

How do you think you might build and maintain a strange workforce? Is it simply luck? Let's just start off by saying it's really unlikely that you can build a strange workforce if your organization deals with the workforce the same way as other organizations do. It is delusional to expect your employees to be extraordinary and differentiate your organization if your employee systems are basically the same as other organizations.

Your workforce systems need to be as strange as the workforce you hope to create. All your people management processes should result in a strange system that gets noticed by employees and makes them obsess on the things that customers care about the most. From this perspective, the processes your organization uses to manage people must be part of your unique way of competing. This means that job applicants and new employees should perceive your people systems as strikingly different and unexpected, slightly odd, and even a bit weird.

> **Your workforce systems need to be as strange as the workforce you hope to create.**

Your people systems should inform employees and potential employees how to act so that customers notice something different and reach for their wallets again and again. For example, your hiring systems should be strange enough that some applicants who go through your process say to themselves, "This organization is too strange for me," and go work somewhere more normal…like your competitors.

As a leader, how do you know whether *your* people systems are set up to do this? You need to gather data that you can use to create your special sauce. And guess what? You can't use the garden-variety HR metrics that most organizations use. For example, there is a wood delivery company with a strategy that its truck drivers develop strong social ties with clients while making deliveries—to develop trust and gather information about upcoming shipment issues. To execute this strategy, the company actually needs to hire customer service reps who happen to drive 18 wheelers as well. Does it make sense for this company to hire normal truck drivers just like all the other trucking companies do, when they want to produce their own special sauce of networking and customer intimacy? Does it make sense for the recruitment metrics to be "cost of hire" and "days position is open?" Does it make sense for the hiring metrics for this job to be "years of trucking experience" and the pay metric to be "market midpoint for truck drivers" when the goal is to hire a strange, rare breed of drivers that is going to help execute a unique strategy? More likely, this company needs to have unique hiring metrics that reveal whether they are hiring drivers who are strangely attracted to a job where they are expected to get to know the plant managers and learn something when they deliver. It might take considerably longer to find that special combination of traits, and you might need to pay substantially more for a customer service rep-turned-trucker.

Doesn't sound like rocket science, does it? In fact, it sounds a lot like common sense. However, this type of system alignment is not very common at all. As you know, the customary practice is for companies to benchmark and use cost controls on people systems so that every company looks and feels to employees like every other company. And from this copycatting, race-to-the-lowest-cost approach to workforce management, a leader expects to produce a rare, unique workforce that will differentiate their company and build a competitive advantage? Good luck with that.

When Strange Turns Normal

Home Depot established a competitive advantage by creating a strange workforce. How was the workforce strange? Home Depot hired building contractors and put them in the aisles to help customers with home improvement problems. For example, Home Depot associates might show customers the right kind of wire needed to run a three-way circuit so that they can walk in one door, turn on the light, then use another switch to turn out the light at another door. They might even sketch the customer a diagram of how the wiring should be run (a Ph.D. does not help me understand this, but I still have the hand-drawn diagram from the Home Depot associate to this day). Or a Home Depot associate might show you which diamond blade works best on a grinder to cut stone (the expensive thin ones are worth it) and talk to you about how to use the grinder (score the stone with the grain about ¼" and then smack it with a hammer and cold chisel). And they might even suggest which thick gloves you should wear.

Helping customers buy the right products and teaching them how to use the products is valuable to consumers because it saves them time (like trips back to the store), prevents costly and dangerous errors, and creates a sense of familiarity and trust with the store. These "contractor grade" associates gave Home Depot a competitive advantage, meaning that people like me would drive a little farther and give this store money because we experienced something different about the store and liked it.

This was a winning practice until Home Depot tried growing at the pace of a new store every week in the midst of a large house-building boom. It became difficult to find enough contractor-grade trades people to put in the aisles. As a consequence, today it is hard for customers to find associates in Home Depot stores who actually have worked in the trades and can solve building problems. Nowadays Home Depot often feels a lot more like most other retailers: IF you can locate (and then chase down) an associate in the store, the most you are going to learn about the product is which aisle you can find it. Nowadays, I shop at Lowe's because it's two miles closer to my house, and I don't notice any difference in the products, price, or advice I get.

Winning Through Measurement

If Home Depot were going to try to win through its strange contractor-grade aisle workers, it might have been useful for Home Depot leaders to obsess on measuring this concept of "contractor grade" and the ratio of contractor-to-noncontractor associates in the aisles. This metric would mean that they would see a "red flag" start flapping when the ratio reached a certain critical low level. This red flag would mean they had to slow down on opening new stores until they could find more contractor-grade associates to put in the aisles—because they weren't creating anything unique anymore.

How would they know how many contractor-grade associates were needed on a shift? It might have been useful for Home Depot leaders to gather data on the percentage of customers who noticed something unique and valuable about Home Depot stores compared to other home improvement stores and correlate this with repeat business. In other words, it might have been useful to determine the contractor-to-noncontractor ratio that was financially doable but that still made customers notice a difference that brought them back again and again. This data would have allowed leaders to link workforce data to a particular competitive strategy and see whether associates were creating a competitive advantage. Figure 1.1 shows an analysis that a leader might want in order to make decisions.

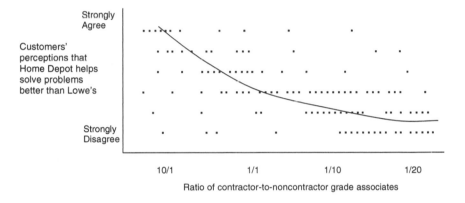

Figure 1.1   How strong does the special sauce need to be to make customers notice?

Of course, actually collecting this data would be annoying and difficult. Store managers would need to agree on what the concept "contractor-grade" really meant and how it could be measured instead of just verbalized. This would mean a lot of arguing in long meetings about applicant testing and whether "contractor-grade" really meant being certified as an electrician or a plumber. Or whether Home Depot could develop its own certification process and test each new hire and then recertify once a year. Essentially, Home Depot would need to get in the business of gathering data on the concept of "contractor-grade" associates. As an intelligent reader, you say: "But this process would be very, very useful for them—after all, this is what they are basing their future on!" Ah, but this would be very, very annoying if you are a store manager and think you have a "real job" to do that doesn't include testing people.

Why else would it be annoying to collect the data in the scatterplot? Home Depot stores would need to assemble accurate data on the number of different types of associates on the floor during different shifts in order to calculate the ratios. But the hiring and the scheduling databases don't currently talk to each other. Stores also would need to collect data from customers about their perceptions of Home Depot versus Lowe's. This might mean having customers answer a question on the checkout screen while swiping their credit card. Stores might need to offer some incentives to get customers to participate, like a dollar off their purchase for answering the question. This might get expensive. Home Depot employees might try to game these numbers, telling customers how to respond or even reaching over and responding for them! As you can see, it's hard to know what to measure, and it's also hard to actually get accurate data. Given all these problems, it is very, very unlikely that these data would ever be gathered.

Unless the leaders of Home Depot were genuinely obsessed with the concept, and they had an almost-physical craving to create a strange contractor-grade workforce that solved customer problems better than anyone else. Unless leaders believed in their hearts they had to have the data in order to win—or even to stay alive long-term. Even though this type of data might be exactly what Home Depot needed to test its strategy and translate its strategy into reality, the data simply would not be collected unless store managers believed in their guts that without it, they will would lose customers to competitors and eventually go out of business. Store managers would figure out a way to get the right data when they believe they need it just as much—or more—than they need 2x4's in Aisle 12. Come to think of it, I think Lowe's sells 2x4's too.

In the example scatterplot given, you might conclude that the strategy is valid but expensive. Customers do in fact notice when Home Depot invests money into putting contractor-grade associates into the aisles, but you need a high ratio of them around for customers to notice. Since contractor-grade associates are much more expensive to hire (about 40% more than average aisle employees), the investment appears to reach its highest leverage at a 3-1 ratio with diminishing returns after that. This data would have helped validate Home Depot's strategy. Validating your strategy of workforce strangeness rather than assuming it is an important step. Don't forget, your data may show you that your strategy is wrong, and customers don't actually care about or even notice what you think is important, in which case your investments would be wasted! This data would help Home Depot manage the specific contractor-grade ratio required to cost-effectively execute its strategy.

> **Validating your strategy of workforce strangeness rather than assuming it is an important step.**

Anybody can talk about a strategy, but it takes a workforce obsessed about something strange to execute a strategy. You will not differentiate your organization in your customers' eyes by talking about strategy in meetings—strategy must be translated into day-to-day, visible artifacts that are palpably different and valuable to customers. And this does not happen by chance or even hoping really hard. This happens through a disciplined process. For example, strategy gets translated into reality when Home Depot leaders have data to show which stores have the right number of contractor-grade associates hired and scheduled at the right times; when store managers walk job applicants through a hiring system where they are taken to a mock house and scored on their ability to locate and fix three plumbing leaks and diagnose and fix four wiring problems.

Business leaders need a way to unpack what should be strange about their workforces to give their organizations a competitive advantage. Translating strategy into reality demands measurement of the key strategic assumptions about people and what customers must notice about them. You should have a way to measure and monitor what your workforce needs to know, act like, or create so that customers notice, reach into their wallets, and say, "I'm giving you my money even though I could get this from many different companies."

Goals of This Book

Many leaders have stories about differentiating and winning, but nobody is really listening to them. There is no discipline to enforce it and make it real. The challenge many leaders face is not developing a strategy, but getting it

> **The challenge many leaders face is not developing a strategy, but getting it translated into reality through their workforces.**

translated into reality through their workforce. Only through a workforce—a group of employees who behave in a strange way that customers appreciate—can a strategy succeed. By translating a strategy into a measurable set of Workforce Deliverables and people management systems, leaders can clarify the thinking of employees and achieve results that customers notice. To this end, the recipe for this book is one part inspiration and two parts practical application.

The goals of this book are

- **To inspire you to build a strange workforce**. Reliably beating the competition into the ground means your workforce has to be strikingly different than your competition. What is your organization's special sauce, and is your workforce strange enough to create it?

- **To introduce the Strange Workforce Value Chain**. This is how to get your story straight about your workforce and why customers notice unique value. It is critical for you to have it clear in your head so that you can make it clear in employees' heads.

- **To help you turn your Strange Workforce Value Chain into a system of metrics**. This lets you steer your organization toward winning and demonstrate you are leveraging your workforce to win in the unique way that you want to win. This brings discipline to fuzzy concepts that are the basis of your competitive advantage.

- **To help you make choices about your workforce systems**. Your workforce systems form an architecture that needs to be as strange as the workforce you want to create. We will work on making system choices that culminate in a strange workforce that provides differentiated behaviors.

I'm Not a CEO. Should I Stop Reading Now?

This book focuses on creating strategy and converting it into reality through measurement. If you are not part of the C-level team, you don't get the chance to select your organization's strategy, and you may not get the chance to select which metrics are used to judge how well the strategy is paying off. I promise this book will be useful to you for two reasons, even if you are not the CEO:

1. As a leader of a sub-organization, you still must create strategy and enact it within the realm of your sub-organization. Sure, you are given (hopefully) the approach your organization is taking to beat the competition. Sure, you are given metrics (hopefully) that your organizational will use to gauge the success of your sub-organization, but then the ball is in your court to figure out how your sub-organization needs to act to achieve the goals you are given. In other words, you need to create your own strategy that defines who your own organization serves, how your own organization creates value, and how your own workforce must be strange to achieve the goals that are given to you. You will need to find a way to communicate your ideas to the workforce that you manage, get them to obsess on converting your strategy into reality, and measure the progress you are making. This book will help you.

2. The process described in point one—articulate a strategy, convert concepts into metrics, build a strange workforce that executes strategy—is a skill. It is not innate. This process can be learned and practiced, and you can get good at it. And when you get good at it, it's valuable. Your organization and many other organizations will value this skill, and you will get promoted to a job where you have more scope, more leverage, and a larger organization to lead. You practice this process some more and get even better at it and get another raise and promotion. Repeat these steps until you are a CEO, if you want.

2

Shine a Flashlight into the Black Box That Exists Between Your Workforce and Beating Your Competition

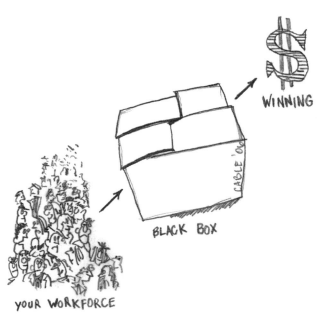

Figure 2.1 Is there mystery between your people and your profit?

A strategy is a theory. It's a theory about what causes what, a series of if-then statements. "If our workforce can produce and offer this unique thing, customers will notice and like it and give us their money." It's a way of stating the kinds of risks that you are going to take to differentiate and build value in customers' minds.

In this chapter, I introduce the overall model you can use to link up your organization's strategy with your people and your people systems. I call this model the *Strange Workforce Value Chain*, and it has three goals. The first is to give you a simple framework for articulating your strategy in terms of your workforce. The Strange Workforce Value Chain helps you be very clear about

You can connect the dots between employees' contributions and your organization's strategy.

how you expect to beat the competition and stir up the special sauce you need from your workforce to make that happen. It helps you be logical when you talk to employees about what you need from them and why you need it. It helps you be a motivating leader because you consistently link employees' behaviors and accomplishments to winning. You can connect the dots between employees' contributions and your organization's strategy.

Being able to *articulate* how your people execute your strategy is necessary but not sufficient. Lots of leaders talk about how they need their workforces to "be close to the customer" and "develop an innovative culture," but nothing really happens (except the employees get more cynical). It's a little like that Seinfeld episode where he reserves a rental car, but when he gets there, they have given the car to someone else. Jerry says anyone can *take* a reservation—the valuable part is the *keeping* the reservation. Likewise, anyone can *talk about* strategy—the valuable part is *executing* the strategy. Research estimates that 70% of business failures are not due to poor strategy; they are due to poor execution.[1, 2]

---

[1] Charan, R., & Colvin, G. 1999. "Why CEOs fail." *Fortune*, June, 21.

[2] Zook, C. 2001. "Profit from the Core: Growth strategy in an era of turbulence." Boston: Harvard Business School Press. The Strategy-Focused Organization.

What I'm saying here is that the first goal—being able to articulate the unique competitiveness concepts and strange behaviors needed from your workforce—is needed but not enough to reach the second goal of the Strange Workforce Value Chain, which is measuring your competitiveness concepts. This next step means strapping numbers onto your concepts of winning so that you can bring discipline to the words that are your strategy. If you can't measure the core concepts of how you intend to win, how will you know whether your workforce actually is doing anything strange? How will you know your customers actually are noticing anything different?

So, the first goal of the Strange Workforce Value Chain is to help you articulate workforce strangeness, and the second is to help you measure the concepts that will make you win. If this is as far as you get, it is probably enough. Accomplishing these two steps is not easy to do, but if you accomplish them, you have a very powerful tool that allows you to manage your investments and your workforce toward strategy execution every day. This usually is enough to put the hurting on your competition because you simply out-perform them. At this point, you have reached the second stage of *Strange Workforce Enlightenment.*

Total enlightenment is still a step away. The third goal of the Strange Workforce Value Chain is to help you *test* your theory about using your workforce to win. By "test" I mean actually running statistics to examine the segments of logic that hold together your theory of beating the competition. Let me make it clear from the get-go that not everyone will be able to test their theories of winning. For example, leaders of small organizations with a single location or owners of mom and pop businesses usually cannot test their theories simply because the sample size is too small to run any statistics. In these small-scale situations, they develop their Strange Workforce Value Chains so that they can tell a clear, consistent, compelling story to their workforces and gather data that lets them focus their workforces and execute their strategies.

But if you lead a large organization with a big workforce and many territories, stores, or sub-organizations, then you have the golden opportunity to literally analyze whether your theory of winning is right. Because guess what? You may find that your ideas of competition are wrong, and customers don't actually notice what *you* think is so important. This sounds like a disaster, but it's invaluable because you have the chance to cut your losses and find something customers do care about before you waste all your money on initiatives that look compelling in your PowerPoint presentation but that customers don't notice.

Organizational changes often are painful, expensive, risky ventures that require changes in workforce behavior. Many organizational changes result in workforce cynicism instead of value creation. Try this on: Rather than just assuming your theory of organizational change is correct and throwing resources at it throughout your organization, try testing it on a subset of your workforce. You win either way. If the data demonstrate your theory of winning is right, you have powerful ammunition to roll it out more deeply into the organization,[3] and you probably have learned a heck of a lot more about your organizational change in the process. If, on the other hand, the data show that your change strategy does not lead to the outcomes you anticipated, you saved your organization the pain, suffering, and financial investment of another failed change initiative.

Let's say you are the leader of a wealth management organization in a large bank. You theorize as part of your change strategy that if you concentrated on higher-wealth individuals, you could turn greater revenues and profits with fewer client interactions and fewer financial consultants. However, to concentrate on really high-wealth clients, you hypothesize your financial consultants would need certain financial knowledge and would need to learn how to interact appropriately with high-wealth clients. This is a theory of change made up of testable questions about how to make your workforce strange, such as:

- When we invest in training our consultants, they are more likely to pass their financial certifications.

- When we invest in training our consultants, they feel more comfortable and capable of interacting with high-wealth individuals.

- High-wealth individuals are more likely to report positive rapport with consultants who have passed their financial certifications and feel comfortable interacting with wealthy individuals.

[3] Kotter, J. P. 1995. "Leading Change: Why transformations efforts fail." *Harvard Business Review*. March-April, 59-67.

- Consultants with financial certifications who report being comfortable interacting with high-wealth individuals spend more time interacting with high-wealth individuals and acquire higher portfolio values.

- Our investments in consultant training correspond with an increase in average portfolio value, translating to greater revenues with fewer consultants.

These hypotheses could be tested at a few locations before rolling out the initiative nationwide. Notice how you need to master the first two goals of the Strange Workforce Value Chain before you can move to Goal Three (Enlightenment). Before you can test anything empirically, you first need to be able to clearly articulate your strategic hypotheses and the way your workforce needs to be strange, and you secondly need to build a process to gather the right data about your competitiveness concepts. As I discussed in the introduction, this will be hell. It will be time-consuming, and it may be expensive and take six tries to get right. Gathering data on your competitiveness concepts is exactly where you should be spending your time if you actually want to create an effective change and understand what adds value in your customers' eyes.

> **Gathering data on your competitiveness concepts is exactly where you should be spending your time if you actually want to create an effective change and understand what adds value in your customers' eyes.**

Valid data is not easy to come by, and it generally is not data that is already being collected. For example, how would you personally measure the "perceived rapport" of high-wealth individuals with their financial consultants? This would take some doing. You could develop a survey (pretty easy) and somehow get a large percentage of the high-wealth clients to answer the survey without bothering them (good luck with that). What if you could gather the data not as part of a "survey" but in a way that was part of a "pleasant touch" interaction with the client? Maybe this would involve a brief telephone call. Or maybe the way to go is a visit from you, a very important person who has better things to do with your time. Or do you? Maybe you would learn the most interesting things about your clients' needs while you were talking with them about what they do and don't like about their financial consultants. Collecting valid data on the key concepts of your organizational change is one of the best uses of your time. At least that is what I'm going to try and convince you of throughout this book.

Bottom line: If you don't have valid data on your concepts, you can't reach the coveted "True Nirvana Stage" of the Enlightenment Pyramid that is shown in Figure 2.2.

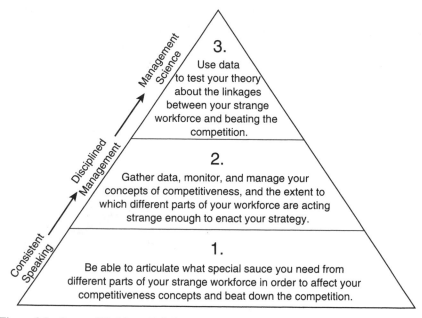

Figure 2.2   Strange Workforce Enlightenment Pyramid

Get on with It. Introduce the Strange Workforce Value Chain Already!

The Strange Workforce Value Chain provides a way to map your theory of winning. There are four distinct steps that help you get your story straight about how you will build a strange workforce so that your employees will differentiate your organization for customers and so that all the money that would go to your competitors comes to you instead.

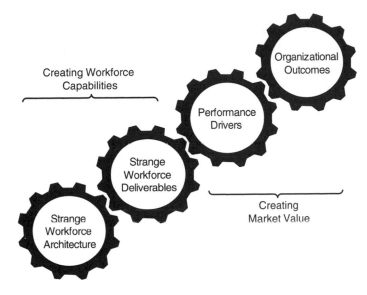

Figure 2.3 Strange Workforce Value Chain

The first two steps deal with how you create value and win in the marketplace. The second two steps deal with how you build a strange workforce with unique capabilities that customers notice and care about. Here is a brief introduction to the four steps that we will tunnel into in Chapters 3 through 9:

Step 1: **Organizational Outcomes**. The Strange Workforce Value Chain begins with the end in mind. Go out three years from now. Imagine a brave new world in which your workforce was strange and you were beating the competition into the ground using your strategy, your unique way of winning. What would be the ultimate results if your strategy paid off big? What are the fruits of your organization's labor over the last three years? What would have changed in the world that you could point to and say, "Look, friend, here is conclusive evidence that our strategy is paying off." These are your Organizational Outcomes, and you only want to have three or four of them. You want to begin with the end in mind because everything your workforce does should be means to those ends. In Chapter 4, "Performance Drivers: What Must Customers Notice to Make Me Win?," we are going to work on getting

> **You want to begin with the end in mind because everything your workforce does should be means to those ends.**

your organizational outcomes down to three or four measures that together give you the evidence you need to demonstrate that your strategy is paying off—or not paying off. Both are important to know.

Organizational Outcomes are *lagging* or *rear-view mirror indicators*. This stuff has already happened. With these data, you might say, "Repeat business has dropped off; our customers went to the competition, and it's too late to stop them now." Lagging indicators are essential but not very proactive, and they don't tell you what to change. Bless your heart if this is all you measure to lead your organization.

Step 2: **Performance Drivers**. Organizational Outcomes are the *results* of enacting your strategy; Performance Drivers are the concepts that *are* your strategy. Performance drivers are the answers to the question, "As an organization, what do we create or provide that is valuable, rare, and hard to imitate?" Performance drivers specify what customers need to notice about your organization in order to make them choose you over your competition. What has to happen for you to get to the end state that you desire? Chapter 4, helps you to develop two or three performance drivers for each Organizational Outcome. And you can't let yourself off the hook with shiny, hollow phrases like "customer intimacy" or "quality." No indeed, you have to dig deep and get messy with collecting valid data that accurately reflect the meaning of your concepts. That data will go into an Excel spreadsheet, and it will allow you to track and manage the extent to which your strategy is being enacted.

You can think of performance drivers as *windshield indicators*. These you see immediately before you. With these data, you might say, "Our customers are beginning to notice something bad about us that doesn't synch up with our strategy; we'd better fix it before they go to our competitors." Windshield indicators are valuable because you still have a little time to avoid a collision, but you need to react quickly, and you may not know which way to turn.

Step 3: **Strange Workforce Deliverables**. This stage of the model deals explicitly with your workforce's special sauce. The focus is on the ways the people in your workforce must be strange to make your Performance Drivers happen and make a positive, unique impression on your customers. Sometimes the deliverables literally pertain to your entire workforce, where every employee in every part of the organization must have a certain obsession. But often *different* deliverables are needed from different parts of the workforce. What is demanded from the aisle associates to differentiate Home Depot is different from what is needed from the marketing managers. Chapters 5 and 6 deal with these issues.

You can think of Strange Workforce Deliverables as *road sign indicators*. These you see as warning you about what is coming up unless you change your course. With these data, you might say, as in the Home Depot example, "We are quickly losing what customers notice as unique! We are no longer putting contractor-grade professionals in the aisles because we are opening up new stores too fast. We need to slow down and execute our strategy if we want customers to notice anything special about us." These data tell you specific information about what you are and are not getting from your workforce, and this is the first pressure point where you can exert some control as a leader and where you have some power to do something about the situation.

Step 4: **Strange Workforce Architecture**. Architecture deals with principles of design and construction. Designing and constructing certain people management systems will make it more likely that your workforce will be strange and make customers notice good things about you. If your people systems (such as recruiting, hiring, socializing, paying, and training) essentially mimic your competitors, it would be silly to expect any special sauce from your workforce. You need to inject some strangeness in your people systems, something that signals loud and clear to people that "…around here we obsess on this thing that customers value, and you shouldn't be here unless that appeals to you." Chapters 7 through 9 discuss the cornerstones of your Workforce Architecture and help you make sure your people systems are, in fact, strange enough to get applicants' and employees' attention, and that they are linked up to the type of workforce results, behaviors, and knowledge that you need.

You can think of Strange Workforce Architecture as *mapping indicators*, helping you plan the route you need to take. With these you might say, "The level of pay that we're offering our aisle associates is about the same as other home improvement stores. Even more troubling, the amount we're offering is 44% *below* what contractor-grade people can make on any construction site. We either need to offer a strikingly large amount of pay for these jobs so we can attract and hire contractor-grade applicants, or we need to figure out a powerful, intense training system to get normal applicants up to contractor-grade status." Mapping indicators are valuable because out of all the steps, you have the most control over these. You get to make decisions about how to hire, how often to have performance management discussions and what to focus on, and how much to pay and how pay is distributed. Sometimes it might not feel like it, but these are levers that organizations control to steer the Workforce Value Chain.

That, in a nutshell, is the Strange Workforce Value Chain. So if you work with me on it, what do you get? You get three of the most important possessions that you can have as a leader:

- **A consistent and compelling story about how your workforce must be unusual or striking to create your competitive advantage and how you can go about getting that workforce.** This book gives you an approach that you can use to craft your own Strange Workforce Value Chain, which is your path to building a great organization.

- **A way to make your strategy concrete for the people who actually have to enact it for customers.** An organization becomes a powerful winning machine when each member locks the competition in his sights, knows how to act in order to take down the competition, and knows what winning looks like. Creating this workforce is your primary job as a leader, but most leaders fail miserably at this main concern. Most employees are not clear on how to prioritize their work, are unsure who their customers are, and are not clear how their jobs or behaviors affect "winning." This book gives you an approach to help your people understand the big picture and how to prioritize their work.

- **An integrated, focused set of metrics that are hell to acquire but that allow you to manage the most vital parts of your strategy.** Measuring your fuzzy concepts of competitiveness is the only way to make sure everyone in the room is talking about the same thing. Strapping numbers onto conceptual ideas is a cornerstone of this book because it creates the discipline it takes to turn strategy into reality. This book presents an approach to developing measures and building processes for getting valid data that let you track and test the key assumptions of your theory of winning.

Fortunately, This Stuff Is Hard to Do

Gosh, writing down those bullets was kind of easy. But actually achieving them as a leader is very hard. Let's take a moment and be grateful for this being very hard. Why? Let me develop an analogy:

I once had a gym teacher who told us, "If you could buy fitness like clothes, everyone would have it." Truth is, physical fitness and health take a lot more than money. You can't imitate physical fitness easily because you need to personally invest effort doing something time-consuming that often does not feel very pleasant. On the sixth repetition of bicep curls, it literally hurts—your biceps and forearms burn. It's annoying, and the mind says, "Why don't we just stop? Call it a day. Hit the showers." But there is a system of thinking that replies, "No, this is good pain. This pain is the whole point of the exercise. This burn means that I'm strengthening my muscles. If I want to be a fit kind of person, then this is what it takes."

In your business, you need to figure out what the good pain is and then build and manage a strikingly different workforce toward those ends, which means more than just talking. What do you want to create that stands out to customers as valuable but that competitors can't easily duplicate? Then measure your competitiveness concepts and make sure you have follow-through on your intentions. Gathering this data will be as painful and annoying as lifting weights—I can guarantee it. Your organization will want to wrap it up and "hit the showers" after a few false starts or when the pain starts.

> **What do you want to create that stands out to customers as valuable but that competitors can't easily duplicate?**

I also can guarantee that measuring and obsessing on these deliverables, rather than just talking about them, is a major part of building the discipline that customers notice and that your competitors will have a difficult time imitating. When the process of performing and measuring your competitive concepts gets painful and annoying and you want to quit, the only real question you need to ask yourself is, "Is this really how we want to win?" If it is, you need to label that burn "good pain."

Make it a goal to identify the "good pain" in your organization; then embrace it and build a business around measuring and executing it. This is what your organization and workforce is willing and able to do that your competitors cannot or will not. Even if you conducted tours of your successful facility for competitors, and even if you showed competitors the amount of time and energy you personally put into finding, managing, and keeping people who are strange like your organization, they would probably not be able to imitate you. It's a lot like telling people who want to lose weight that they should "eat less and exercise more."

> **Make it a goal to identify the "good pain" in your organization; then embrace it and build a business around measuring and executing it.**

This statement is factual, and it's easy to say, but it's hard to actually do. It takes a lot of discipline, and it hurts to put up with hunger.

Whatever your business does to create a competitive advantage will be tough to achieve. This is why it can be a competitive advantage. If it were easy, everyone would be doing it. Developing your Strange Workforce Value Chain can help you when the going gets tough for two reasons:

- **First, it lets you clearly understand why the pain is worth embracing.** It gives you the story and the strategic reason for the pain that comes from building a strange workforce and performing in ways that customers value but competitors have a hard time replicating.

- **Second, it brings the discipline of measurement to your competitiveness concepts in a way that makes them concrete for employees and manageable to you.** Your workforce starts to become strangely intense about things that customers value.

I believe this is how great organizations become great organizations. They take a decent strategy, develop and work a Strange Workforce Value Chain, and they become a competition machine. You can create an organization that customers notice and competitors fear.

> **You can create an organization that customers notice and competitors fear.**

The next section of this book (Chapters 3 through 9) is focused on making the Strange Workforce Value Chain a valuable, usable tool for you. Chapter 10, "The Magic of Metrics: Creating and Implementing Measurement Systems," focuses on how you convert the fuzzy concepts of your strategy into metrics that you use to build your strange workforce and guide your organization to greatness. I put this as the last chapter because I want to create the *need* to measure stuff before I drag you through the *how* to measure stuff. But if at any time you feel the need to know more about how to measure the strange concepts of your strategy, you can jump to Chapter 10 and read it as background before returning to the Value Chain chapters.

3

Organizational Outcomes: How Do I Know I Am Winning in the Way I Want to Win?

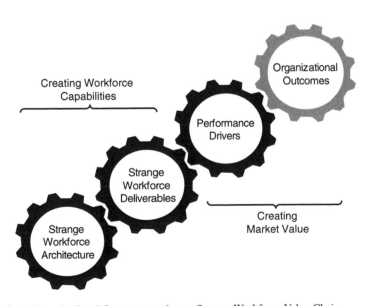

Figure 3.1   Organizational Outcomes and your Strange Workforce Value Chain

Are you able to clearly see the way the world will look when your strategy pays off and you have put the hurtin' on your competitors? Without a clear vision of what winning looks like, you and your workforce have to deal with the pain of doing something hard and often painful without knowing why. That's not very motivating. It's hard to sustain.

> **Without a clear vision of what winning looks like, you and your workforce have to deal with the pain of doing something hard and often painful without knowing why.**

Organizational Outcomes are what you measure to know whether you are winning in the way you want to win. Imagine what the world will look like when you are winning through your strange workforce. Picture it: You are beating the competition into the ground using your unique way of winning. Now, what can you measure to prove it? Point to something that will happen in the world and say, "This will be evidence that our strategy is paying off."

Don't Confuse Means with Ends

Why does your organization exist? What are you in the business of producing? If you think of everything your organization does and creates as *means*, Organizational Outcomes are the *ends*.

This may not seem like a complicated idea, but lots of leaders seem confused by it. When I ask leadership teams how they know if they are winning, they often talk about their workforce. They say with pride that they know they are winning because "the best and the brightest work here" or "our turnover rate is under 5%." These are not ends (the reason the organization exists). Unless the reason for your organization's existence is to hire and pay people, your workforce is a means to an end, a vehicle to take you to your goals, not an end unto itself. Means and ends are easy to confuse because you need them both, and they are connected. But when it comes to articulating and testing your theory of winning, it's important to keep means and ends separate. You need to be able to track whether or not you are winning.

Your Organizational Outcomes are the numbers that represent the ultimate result of your business. To create your Strange Workforce Value Chain, start with the end in mind because the particular way that your workforce needs to be strange depends on what you are trying to accomplish. Our goal in this chapter is to develop three or four metrics that, as a system, represent the success of your organization. What you track and measure as your Organizational Outcomes should not be generic. They should reflect the results of your organization's unique goals and strategy. If you use stock price and profits as your Organizational Outcomes, you are probably in trouble. These outcomes may indeed be evidence that you are winning, but they probably do not prove that you are winning in the way you want to win.

> **To create your Strange Workforce Value Chain, start with the end in mind because the particular way that your workforce needs to be strange depends on what you are trying to accomplish.**

Sticky Situation

Let's say that it is 1980 and 3M just started marketing the sticky note. The little patented notes are selling like hotcakes, and they are a blockbuster new product. You are hired as the president of 3M. You are told that the Organizational Outcomes are stock price and profitability. That is, your success as a leader will be judged by your ability to grow stock price and increase profits.

So you come into the organization and start looking around. You see that you have these sticky pads selling like mad with patent protection. That's nice. You also see that you have all these research engineers, expensive people, with their research-y Ph.D.s. They are a strange group. They spend a lot of time thinking and talking, and half the stuff they invent never ends up going to market. They seem to waste a lot of time on rogue "bootleg projects" that are not even part of their job descriptions.[1] These engineers and their invention labs are costing 3M a ton of money.

---

[1]   Business Week Online. April 24, 2006. http://www.businessweek.com/magazine/content/06_17/b3981401.htm.

So in order to win, here is what you decide to do: You fire two-thirds of the bench engineers. To push sales, you put a quarter of the newfound money into umbrella branding and marketing the sticky note so that you create pink ones, ones with lines, really little ones, and some larger ones. You put a quarter of the found money into shareholder dividends, to drive up the stock price. You let the rest of the found money ride as profit. Now you have a situation where costs are lower, profitability is increased, and stock is trading higher. Your Organizational Outcomes show you that you are winning, right? Surely, increasing stock price and profits are things that any organization would be thrilled with, right?

Maybe not. Is 3M really in the business of sticky pad production and distribution? No, 3M is an invention shop. The soul of the organization, the reason why 3M exists and the way that it stays alive and relevant over the decades, is by inventing new things that its customers want. Why wouldn't your actions be appropriate as a 3M president? Because in ten years, long after you personally have been hired away by another organization, 3M wouldn't have any new products to take to market. The Organizational Outcomes of profitability and stock price appreciation made you obsess on the wrong goals and encouraged you to behave in a way that was counter to 3M's unique way of winning.

In 2006, *Business Week* ranked 3M as the third "Most Innovative Company" in the world (they were ranked #2 in 2005). 3M also is a perennial favorite in *Fortune's* "Ten Most Admired Corporations."[2] Even as a huge company, 3M has remained innovative and carried a stream of new products into many different industries ranging from Medical to Automotive, from Electronics to Office Supply, and from Dental to Industrial Coatings. What is one of their key Organizational Outcomes? Not *profits* per se, but *profits from products that were invented within four years*.

To me, this seemingly small shift in an Organizational Outcome metric is very dramatic and exciting. Why? Because we know that people are deeply affected by what is measured. Because it is not profits, but profits from products that were invented within four years, that provides a valid reflection of

---

[2]   Bartlett, C. A. & Mohammed, A. 1995. "3M: Profile of an innovating company." Harvard Business School, 9-395-016; *Fortune* article.

winning for 3M. It is not generic—it maps onto 3M's reason for existing as an organization. It reflects the way 3M *intends* to win—through superior product invention. If you were the 3M President and winning was all of a sudden not represented by profits, but instead by profits from products invented in the last four years, you would never sell out the research engineers because now they are your tap root, your saviors. Instead of cutting them, you would be spending a lot of time with them, trying to understand, manage, and improve the pipeline of their future inventions. You would obsess on tracking which new products have passed through the final stages of testing and approval and are ready to be marketed and sold the following year. You would lose sleep worrying about what looks possible over the next two to three years—"what are my solid base hits for 2008 that I can count on, what are my 'swing for the seats' products for 2008 that could be the next sticky pad?" You would obsess about the product pipeline and invest lots of energy and resources making sure the right engineers were on the benches and that they were engaged and committed to inventing and making 3M win. You would build an organization that was as obsessed about new product innovation and going to market as you (3M invests in R&D about twice as much as the average U.S. industrial company). In order to hire and motivate true scientist-inventors who really bring their best to the workplace, you might endorse strange concepts like "bootleg project time" that lets research engineers work on stuff that really interests them. There would be alignment between your theory of winning and your metrics.

It may sound strange for an industrial manufacturer, but 3M spent $1.24 billion on research and development in 2005, or about 6% of its $21.2 billion in revenue. Strangely enough, $248,000,000 of those dollars went to basic research or pursuits that have no immediate practicality. "If you're going to be an innovative company," said Larry Wendling, Vice-President of 3M's corporate research labs, "organic growth and new products have to be what drives the company."[3]

---

[3] Arndt, M. 2006. "3M's Seven Pillars of Innovation," *Business Week*. May 10.

We're Not 3M. What Are Our Organizational Outcomes?

Fair enough. The 3M story whets your appetite to be strategic about your own metrics and shows how seemingly good Organizational Outcomes can lead to wrong behaviors if they are not customized to your unique way of winning. But the story does not tell you what *you* should be measuring. Unfortunately, I can't tell you—if it were that easy, it wouldn't be worth reading an entire book about it and couldn't bring you a competitive advantage anyway. But I can give you the process and questions that can get you to the right Organizational Outcomes and that ultimately can result in a competitive advantage.

So here's where you start. Put together a day-long meeting with your top leaders across functions. The entire focus of this meeting is to convert your strategy into a family of three to four measures that together demonstrate that your unique way of winning is paying off. By the end of the meeting, everyone in the room has to agree that, like it or not, these outcomes would indeed be evidence that your special way of beating the competition was working. Everyone should be willing to say, "Everything that we all do every day within every function should add up to us winning in this way." You should not be surprised if this meeting takes eight to ten hours, and you should not be surprised if it is painstaking, onerous, and creates much disagreement.

Have a Good Fight

What happens when leaders talk about how they actually should measure strategic concepts? In my experience, they fight. You and your leadership team probably will fight about which measures to use to reflect your competitiveness concepts. Even if you think you all agree about your strategy at the level of "concepts," there will be considerable disagreement when you try to convert your strategic concepts into measures. Some of this fighting will occur because each person views the strategic concepts from his or her own silo (marketing, operations, R&D) rather than organizationally (get noticed by customers, beat competition). When it comes time to collect the data, people see how it will or will not involve their own silos, and it will question some basic assumptions they were working with. As Huckleberry Finn said, "It ain't regular."

As a consultant, I once was afraid when leadership teams started fighting about metrics. Now I understand that this fighting is one of the most important parts of the process, maybe as important as actually gathering the data because it makes leaders come to grips and agree about what their competitiveness concepts do and don't mean. I'd go as far as to say that if you can't all agree on how to *measure* a competitiveness concept, then you don't really know what you mean by the concept. It's essential to agree about what winning looks like if you all are going to pull the oars in the same direction. If your leadership team doesn't know what you mean by winning, how can you explain it to the workforce? How can you get a workforce to enact it?

For example, it's one thing to say you want to be a "top business school." Even a bunch of professors can all agree with that, just as everybody can agree that good is good. It's another thing altogether to say how you are going to measure whether you are a top business school—is it the *Business Week* rankings? Is it the GMAT scores of MBA students? Is it how recruiters rate the MBAs they hire? Sure, all of these measures could be said to reflect winning, but they are very different cuts at the concept, and they have very different implications for the ways that the workforce should be strange, and which unique behaviors the workforce should perform.

Choosing measures to represent your concepts crystallizes the meaning of the concepts and lays bare the assumptions that different leaders are making about the concepts. In this sense, strapping a measure onto a concept helps you clarify your thinking about what you really do mean by it—how it looks or acts in the real world. Choosing measures forces disagreements onto the table to be dealt with rather than everybody agreeing that "good is good" at the conceptual level or letting leaders "agree to disagree." Get it fixed in your head that fighting about metrics is a good thing. It means that you are taking them seriously.

There are four sets of questions that you should focus your leadership team on to expose your Organizational Outcomes. You'll find it useful to iterate back and forth between the questions.

- Who do we serve? Who is our target customer? In what arena will we be most active?

- Who else is trying to serve our target customer? Who or what is threatening our existence as an institution? Who or what is our competition, and what do we take from them when we beat them into the ground?

- What do we do that is strange? What outcomes are we willing to pursue that our competitors would classify as dumb? What risks are we willing to take that other businesses think are not worth taking?

- What three to four pieces of evidence or trends would allow us to claim "we're winning doing it our way" in three to five years?

These are alarmingly simple questions. They seem simple because each person in the room probably feels the answers are obvious. And this is what makes them alarming—everyone thinks he or she already knows the answers, but different leaders have different answers. These questions generally create useful arguments and expose confusion between leaders. Let's look a little more closely at each of the questions and delineate what you want to get out of them during your meeting.

Question Set 1: The Customer and the Marketplace

- *Who do we serve?*

- *Who is our target customer?*

- *In what arena will we be most active?*

The goal of this first set of questions is to make your group have an objective, forthright discussion about who your organization exists to serve. Make sure you agree about what niche you are most interested in staking out for your own and making a mark, because you can't know if you are winning if you don't know who you are serving. Your Organizational Outcome metrics should be evidence that you are providing your targeted customers something distinctive that they need, that you are succeeding in your intended niche.

The more specific you can be about the particular group that you are trying to serve, the more tailored and specific you can develop your metrics of success with that group. For example, Best Buy wants to sell electronics to consumers, right? Well, no, actually—they don't want to serve all customers, as odd as that might sound at first blush.[4] They actually are not very interested in selling to low-value customers, the ones who come into the store but only to buy the lowest profit products (loss leader). Some customers spend lots of time talking to salespeople, but they buy the thing with the least profit, and then they often bring it back a few weeks later, and the store has to eat the restocking fee. This is not a good customer. A good customer buys high-end items with nice fat juicy margins and doesn't return them. So if Best Buy is going to be most active in this "good customer" segment and find out if they are winning, they need to build a business around measuring their results in attracting and retaining this specific market segment. Tracking profits won't offer much granularity about their specific strategy or their success at executing it.

Leaders in charge of different functions often have different perspectives on who the customer is and who the organization is built to serve. All of the leaders in the Bureau of Naval Personnel knew that the goal was to put the right person in the right place at the right time. But some of the leaders viewed the customer as the commanding officers who had open positions (billets) and needed people deployed to the positions. Other leaders focused on the American Sailor as the customer because the Navy is an all-volunteer force, and unless people reenlisted there wouldn't be much of a force. Still others focused on the American Taxpayer as the customer, and helping the Navy accomplish its goals with less workforce so that funds could be freed up to recapitalize the fleet (buy new ships with better technology). All of these perspectives are accurate, and each of these constituents must be considered. However, a leader operating in a given silo of your organization may "live to serve" one specific customer type and might view that customer type as the center of the universe, considering that is his or her daily focus. The

---

[4]   McWilliams, G. 2004. "Minding the Store: Analyzing Customers, Best Buy Decides Not All Are Welcome." *Wall Street Journal* (Eastern edition). Nov 8: A.1.

way this leader judges his or her own success may not incorporate multiple perspectives nor be aligned with the overall goal and strategic focus of the broader organization. This is *suboptimization*, and it is more common than sense. Conscious, mindful, strategic decisions need to be made about the prioritization of the customers you serve because prioritization affects both how you collect Organizational Outcome data and how you evaluate whether you are winning.

Question Set 2: Competitor Awareness

- *Who else is trying to serve our target customer?*

- *Who or what is threatening our existence as an institution?*

- *Who or what is our competition, and what do we take from them when we beat them into the ground?*

The point with this set of questions is to figure out who or what could serve your intended customers better than you and take them from you. When it comes to the competition, get mad and take it personally. If you want to win, it helps to get yourself and your organization obsessed, paranoid, and worried about the competition that could make you lose. Make it a practice to actually imagine your competition stealing your customers and bleeding your business until you are forced to stop operating. Try to lock that image in your mind's eye and revisit it often. Communicate it to employees and make them know what they can do about it in their jobs. It's useful and motivating to be scrappy and angry about the competition. So what if your organization exists to sell computer software and not cure cancer...given that you're not curing cancer, do you want to beat your competitors or lose to them? If you don't really care that much, you're probably going to lose to them.

> **Make it a practice to actually imagine your competition stealing your customers and bleeding your business dry until you are forced to stop operating.**

Some industries and organizational functions have better competitor awareness than others. From a motivational perspective, the best competitive situation is one in which you see your competition every day. You see them driving their delivery trucks and running their ads, you steal some of their customers, or you lose some of your customers to them. I say this is the best situation because it puts a sharp point on what you must do that is strange (extraordinary, not normal, remarkable) in order to get and keep customers and what this means for your workforce. This sort of hand-to-hand business combat is the most exhilarating because the competition has a face, and the competitive juices get you riled up and make you nervous about losing market share. Your sense of urgency goes up, and it motivates you to come in a little earlier, get it done a little sooner, and make that call instead of putting it off until tomorrow.

But what happens when you run a public water utility? NOW who is your competition? If Joe Public Customer wants to take a shower, he pretty much has to pay you for water, right? Or what if your organization is a government agency? If you lead the Bureau of Naval Personnel, is Kelly Services really going to come in and take over the business of sourcing and deploying sailors? If you lead the Navy JAG Corps, is the commanding officer of a fleet really going to hire a DC law firm when he needs legal advice? What if you lead a cost center within an organization—what if you run the audit group or the HR function? Sure, you can identify your customers, but who or what is your competition? If Organizational Outcome metrics are measures that provide evidence that you are beating your competition, what exactly is the competition?

This is a problem because it's harder to think and act competitively when you can't really see your opposition, and leadership turns out to be a much less interesting process when you can't identify competitors. So here are three tricks that might help you out if you don't think that you have any competition:

1. **The past.** Think about your organization's past performance and results as its competition. How has your organization used resources in the past to achieve results that matter? How can you do better and become much more valuable to your customers? How can you go from being a "current vendor" to becoming "simply indispensable" to

the people you serve? Or how can you maintain the services you currently provide with fewer resources but not drop in quality?

2. **Private industry.** Maybe not now, maybe not next year, but society has a way of changing. Water utilities could be privatized like the trucking industry. Lots of government organizations might be outsourced within a decade or two, although it might seem unthinkable now. Your goal as a leader is to lead your organization a decade into the future, not just next year. Pretend that private industry was here now, trying to put you out of business. What competitive advantage would you have over them? How can you develop and get better at that competitive advantage now? How can you become unassailable?

3. **Irrelevance and non-existence.** Long term, society might not even need a separate force called the Navy if the Army and the Air Force can do what we need with less resources. Get focused on making your organization's products and services so valuable and unique that not only do you not become irrelevant, you become recognized as the standard setter within the function or the industry in which you operate. Despite being a cost-center, maybe your organization's external visibility could boost the external reputation of your whole organization when it is written up in the *Wall Street Journal* as world-class.

The three ideas just listed are just mental exercises that you can use to feel threatened and to take winning seriously—first in your own head, then in your leadership team, and then in your workforce. Unless you have a sense of who or what you are fighting, it's difficult to build much thrill into the process of leading and winning. It's harder to motivate yourself and your workforce that you need to be making your customers say "Wow!" after they interact with you.

If you don't like my ideas for understanding your competitive threats, make up your own. But if you can't come up with a good, clear sense of what the competition is and what is threatening you, I see three possible next steps for you:

1. Put this book down and go watch TV. If you don't care a lot about competing and creating a winning organization, the rest of this book is not going to be much help to you. It probably won't be that much fun or useful to read. It will make a nice coaster for your lemonade.

2. Put this book down and talk to your boss and your boss's boss until you *do* understand what is threatening your organization's existence over the next 10 years and who the competition is.

3. If you really can't come up with anything, and you don't like TV, and you want to become a better leader and create a great organization, start or find an organization where the outcomes matter to you and you can personally feel the threat of competition.

Question Set 3: The *Change* to Strange

- What do we do that is strange?

- What outcomes are we willing to pursue that our competitors would classify as dumb?

- What risks are we willing to take that other businesses think are not worth taking?

This set of questions helps you and your leadership team talk—and fight— about how your organization differentiates itself. Your discussion should deal directly with the way your organization will "cut through the clutter" of the competition and make your target customers notice you, causing them to deposit their money with you.

There are two goals of this set of questions. First, make sure all the members of your leadership team understand the ways in which your strategy is risky. If there aren't any risks to your strategy, then customers probably aren't going to notice it. In other words, if you can't point to the

> **First, make sure all the members of your leadership team understand the ways in which your strategy is risky.**

gamble that you are making or what you are over-investing in, then your strategy is probably not going to differentiate your organization.

Remember, acting just like your competitors *is* very risky; it only feels safe because no one is laughing at you. When no one is laughing at you, you are probably pursuing opportunities that are fairly valued by the market. You want pursue opportunities that are overvalued by customers and/or undervalued by competitors. If the pain of being laughed at is worse for you than the gain of making the best move, then you probably can be a good manager but not a great leader.

A main goal of this set of questions is to make sure that you bake your special sauce and your unique strategy into your family of Organizational Outcome metrics. You should not be chasing identical results as your competition unless you plan to simply out-perform them using their strategy. If you are not chasing the exact same customer base or following the same strategy as your competitors, then what you measure as Organizational Outcomes should reflect what is strange about your organization's approach to winning.

Dumb and Dumber

I started a little toner cartridge company when I was in grad school at Cornell University. My mission was to try and get every laser printer on the Cornell campus to have one of my toner cartridges in it. Because my wife took a job as support staff at Cornell while I attended grad school, I gained some interesting insights into my target market, which was primarily support staff with printers sitting in their offices.

Perhaps the single most important thing I learned was that being on the Preferred Vendor list was very, very important to my target customers. They hated dealing with "limited orders" because it made ordering and paying much harder for them, personally. Gaining access to that Preferred Vendor list let me set up standing purchase orders, which was a competitive advantage that allowed me beat down many of my toner cartridge competitors. To be added to the Preferred Vendor list, I needed to get a sizable number of Cornell's laser printer owners to vouch for my company to General Stores and commit to buying my cartridges into the future.

Another thing I learned that sort of seems obvious now is that many University support employees don't really care if a toner cartridge costs $6 more because it really isn't their money anyway. Many of my target customers were just not all that price sensitive. If the cartridges were easy to buy and printed well, and you gave them a remarkable interaction, that was way more important than a few dollars. The way for me to win was not going to be a race to the lowest price like many of my competitors.

Finally, I learned that amazingly tight social networks exist between support staff in a university building—tighter than you might think. Many of them talk every day if not more often, and if you can find a way to give them a remarkably positive interaction as part of your toner cartridge delivery, or even as part of your sales, there is a decent chance they will mention it to other support staff who eventually need toner cartridges. Let's just say that when you try to sell a cartridge to someone in the Engineering quad and they smile and say, "Actually, Bruce told me about you…," you know you are doing something right.

Anyway, my start-up strategy was basically to make support staff want to say positive things to General Stores and to their friends in the building about my company, become a Preferred Vendor of toner cartridges to support staff, and charge more than my competitors (about $6 more, or 10%, on average). Based on this approach, my primary Organizational Outcome was probably not something my competitors even tracked. My primary Organizational Outcome was not profit, sales volume, or revenue growth. My primary Organizational Outcome—the thing I obsessed on every day—was "number of customers who would vouch for me to General Stores."

We used a simple but very time-consuming procedure to chase this Organizational Outcome. I created a field in my customer database called "date last contacted." Every morning I performed a search in this field for "greater than 30 days." Then I or one of three employees stopped by, in person, to see each of the customers who had not been visited for 30 days. Not to sell anything to them, but just to visit briefly, get a little face time, and ask how they were doing. We made it a point to learn one new thing about them with each visit (customer fun facts), which we entered into that customer's "fun facts field" in the database when we got back to the car. Naturally, we reviewed each customer's existing fun facts immediately before going in for our monthly visit.

We tried to be remarkable, and we tried to we get customers to smile. We tried to be strange. We often told them a joke. (How do you get an elephant out of a subway? Here's a hint: remove the "s" off of "sub." Now remove the "f" off of "way.") Obviously this process didn't work for everyone, but across 12 months, we developed some truly outstanding interpersonal relationships with many customers. How solid? Well, I got calls from my customers saying, "The guy from Laser Exchange came by again today with his sales sheet and another free sample cartridge...do you want these?" Let's just say the relationships were solid enough that they went the extra mile for me in terms of getting me on that Preferred Vendor list. At our request—when the relationship was tight enough—they wrote letters to General Stores vouching for my quality, responsiveness, and value. Some of them personally called important people at General Stores (part of their social network) and told them that their lives would be easier if we were added to the Preferred Vendor list.

Sounds good, right? Why would my competitors think my Organizational Outcome was dumb? Well, remember that my competitors were chasing normal things like profits and revenue growth; they were not strange like us. Lots of the customers we dutifully visited each month only used two cartridges in a year, and our profit margin was only about $18 per cartridge before subtracting costs of doing business. These friendly customer visits probably did not look like a good use of time and money if you are obsessed on revenue and profits. What seemed smart to my competitors? To take a quick drive up into Cornell University and sell to the largest, most profitable customers that used 20-30 cartridges each month (Law School, Vet School, Business School) and then do the same at Ithaca College, and Elmira College, and Binghamton University. If our competitors knew we were spending our time "visiting" a customer 12 times a year—not even hard-selling!—who was only worth $36/year, they would have smiled a gentle smile and said, "Bless their hearts! Look at them, telling their little jokes and typing their little fun facts into a computer. Good luck with that!"

Was my Organizational Outcome dumb? Not to me because it made me execute my unique strategy. It made me obsess on the "right" goals, behaviors, and investments based on my unique approach to winning. I never would have been able to justify the time and resource investment it took to get my "voucher" customers if I had judged the success of my business based on profits per customer, quarterly profits, or even revenue growth. It also worked—in the sense that I was added to the official Preferred Vendor list about a year after starting operations, and then both my direct sales and my unsolicited sales really took off. The networking paid off: Once you get Mary in Agricultural Economics and Tom in Agricultural Extension to be your buddies, using your cartridges and laughing at your jokes, you'd be surprised at how many other laser printer users in the Ag Quad you can bring on board. All just using four or five cartridges per year, all more than willing to spend an extra $6 per cartridge.

My little business taught me a lot about how hard it is to build a strange workforce that customers notice. But my point here certainly is not to get you to start up a toner cartridge business, nor to get you to use the "customer delight" service model. My point is that your Organizational Outcomes need to reflect your own special way of winning, whatever you choose that to be. What you measure will become what you obsess on. You need to obsess on the right things that represent winning based on your unique strategy, that drive the strange behaviors and investments so that your target customers notice you and give you their money. When you tailor your Organizational Outcomes to your strategy, there is a good chance you and your workforce will end up obsessing on things your competitors don't think too much about because they are chasing something else. You and your workforce should act in ways your competitors would not think of duplicating. Your organization will become strange: "out of the ordinary; unusual or striking; differing from the normal." And you want it that way.

> **When you tailor your Organizational Outcomes to your strategy, there is a good chance you and your workforce will end up obsessing on things your competitors don't think too much about because they are chasing something else.**

Question 4: Winning Your Way

- *What three to four pieces of evidence or trends would allow us to claim, "We're winning doing it our way," in three to five years?*

Answering this last question is the culmination, the quest of the entire meeting. You have not finished until you have distilled everything your organization exists to create into three or four metrics. Chapter 10, "The Magic of Metrics: Creating and Implementing Measurement Systems," at the end of this book uses lots of examples in describing the process of going from a theory to data. It may make sense to go read that chapter now; I'll wait for you. Anyway, take the process I describe in Chapter 10 and blend in your leadership team's discussion of the questions just covered. Roast in an oven of disagreement for nine hours. Using this recipe, you want to produce a system of three or four measures that together represent the way the world looks when your targeted customers are served and your competitors are beat, using your unique strategy. Then all leaders across all functions need to do their part to maximize those Organizational Outcome metrics.

Less Is More

You might be saying to yourself, "Our company measures *way* more than three or four Organizational Outcomes. We must be doing a *great* job with metrics!" This is one of those areas where more is decidedly not better. Why? Two reasons:

1. **Everything can't be most important.** The whole point of choosing three to four Organizational Outcomes is that you need to boil everything your organization does into a few numbers that you, your management team, and your workforce can obsess on daily. If you are trying to measure and manage everything, you are not going to be able to obsess on any of them. You want focus.

2. **Measuring things right takes lots of energy and investment.** When you measure lots of Organizational Outcomes, you are probably wasting a lot of energy and money, and you probably are measuring lots of the wrong things poorly. What you want to invest your resources into is measuring the few most important things in a valid way.

Invite Antagonistic Metrics to the Party

No metric is an island. The process of picking metrics works better when you think about *systems* or *families* of metrics, rather than thinking about metrics in isolation. So as you distill your theory of winning into measurements, you need to inject the concept of "antagonistic metrics." Your goal is to measure multiple competitiveness concepts that fight each other, that are at odds with each other—this is what I mean about them being antagonistic. One way to think of this is to picture your body lifted by pulleys on the ceiling with a single length of rope. The rope is attached to your ankles, your wrists, and your head. The goal is to keep your body straight. You can't drop your feet because it will yank up your arms. You can't raise your arms because the rope will go slack, and your head will fall down. The system monitors itself; it doesn't let you cheat.

String up your organization with an antagonistic system of metrics. For example, GE's Durham Engine Facility measures success with four antagonistic metrics:

- On-time delivery

- Number of defects

- Cost

- Safety

Sure, the assembly teams could reduce their costs by hiring fewer people and getting more hours out of the existing trained teams...but accidents go up when people work too many long, intense hours. Sure, a team could get an engine done ahead of schedule if they rushed and were careless...but then defects and accidents would increase. These four metrics together form a system of measurement greater than the sum of the individual metrics because each "keeps the other honest." Together, this system of measures represents success of each team and of the facility as a whole. If a group or a member cheats on one of the metrics, they pay for it in another metric. As you are developing your own measurements, keep in mind that they are an interrelated system and look for metrics that antagonize each other to prevent suboptimization.

Does It Make Sense to Boil It All Down to One Single Success Metric?

Some leaders like the simplicity of creating a single ratio that represents organizational success. For example, GE's Durham Engine Facility could take their four Organizational Outcomes of cost (dollars under/over budget), on-time delivery (days missed), safety (OSHA reportables and near misses), and quality (defects per unit shipped) and convert them into:

Success = (Quality – Delivery) / (Cost + Safety)

On the one hand, I don't like the melding together of Outcomes because it hides information. On the other hand, you can always unpack the information and there are some benefits of a single index. For example, because a single metric packs a lot more information into a single number, it makes it easier to communicate, and it makes goal setting easier to implement.[5] Trying to integrate three or four pieces of data into a single ratio also can be a useful exercise for your leadership team because it demands that you make explicit decisions about the relative importance of each individual metric and if any elements should be weighted more than other elements. A single number also can be used as a motivational tool because it sends a signal to everyone that we are all working toward one goal. One leader I work with sends a single number that represents his entire organization's success to every employee in the organization, every morning.

What Happens to Our Organizational Outcomes Metrics When We Change Our Strategy?

I know you already know the answer to this. Deep in your heart, you know that when the strategy changes, your metrics need to change too. There is probably nothing more futile, or more common, than changing the strategy but keeping the metrics of success the same. Why is it futile? Because your old metrics will continue to drive the old behaviors, and your new strategy needs new behaviors. Why is it common? Because the old metrics are

---

[5] Peeples, D. E. 1978. "Measure for productivity." *Datamation*, 24: 222-230; Pritchard, R. D., Jones, S. D., Roth, P. L., Stuebing, K. K., & Ekeberg, S. E. 1989. "The evaluation of an integrated approach to measuring organizational productivity." *Personnel Psychology*, 42, 69-115.

comfortable. People in your organization (including you) have created patterns of behavior that seem nice because you don't have to think about them too much any more. Change is hard, and we know that most organizational changes don't work.[6] These are good reasons to not try to implement an organizational change in the first place. But what I'm saying here is that

> **There is probably nothing more futile or more common than changing the strategy but keeping the metrics of success the same.**

once you *do* decide to implement an organizational change, then your Organizational Outcome metrics must change to reflect your new way of winning.

Where Do We Go from Here?

When you measure three or four Organizational Outcomes and start to take them seriously, you will become motivated to build an organization around creating success on those measures. The next chapter of this book focuses on articulating and measuring the Performance Drivers of your Organizational Outcomes.

---

[6]   Kotter, J. P. 1995. "Leading Change: Why transformations efforts fail." *Harvard Business Review*. March-April, 59-67.

4

Performance Drivers: What Must Customers Notice About Us So That We Win?

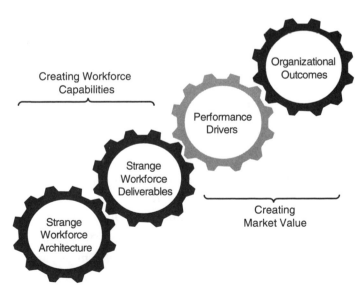

Figure 4.1 Performance Drivers and your Strange Workforce Value Chain

What has to happen to get to that end state you desire? Performance Drivers are what cause your Organizational Outcomes to move; they specify what customers need to notice and think about your organization in order to make them choose you over your competition. In this chapter, I argue that you should literally build your organization around measuring and gaming your Performance Drivers, which results in a strange workforce. Developing, measuring, and enacting your Performance Drivers will not be easy (fortunately!), but it will give you incredible insight into what your organization is creating and not creating in order to differentiate you, attract customers, and win. It will bring discipline to the words and ideas that are your strategy, and you will be able to track and manage the extent to which your strategy is being enacted. You know you want this; the only question is how hard are you willing to work to get it?

Games People Play

As the Dean of a business school, you decide that the best reflection of winning is *Business Week*'s rankings. These are prominent reputation scores created by a third party that directly pits business schools against each other every two years. Essentially all MBA applicants know about the *Business Week* rankings, and the smartest MBA applicants with highest motivation try to go to the best-ranked schools. If you attract really smart, motivated people to your school and simply don't mess them up too bad, there is a very good chance they will go out and succeed in their careers. And then guess where they will want to hire their future MBAs? In fact, loyalty aside, most successful companies want to recruit MBA students from schools with the best public reputations. And who can command the highest salaries and the best jobs from these great companies? You've got it: MBAs graduating from the top-ranked programs. These virtuous cycles are why you picked *Business Week*'s rankings as your primary Organizational Outcome.

Do you want to know what your Performance Drivers are? Then you need to call *Business Week*. Because once you selected these particular rankings as the evidence that will let you know that you are winning, the only way to learn your Performance Drivers is to figure out how *Business Week* creates the rankings. So you call up *Business Week* and learn the formula. Forty-five percent of the ranking is based on what your MBAs say about your school after they have been in the program a year. Forty-five percent of the ranking is based on what the companies that hire your MBA students say about your school. That leaves 10%—what is that extra 10%? That's just a little remainder, hardly worth thinking about too much, but that is your school's "Intellectual Capital." But Intellectual Capital sounds sort of important for a university, right? How is that measured? There is a list of 18 business publications that are considered important by *Business Week*, and each time one of your faculty members publishes a paper in one of those, your school gets a point.

So now that you know the determinants of winning, how do you want to go about gaming these Performance Drivers? One thing is sure: You have little need to worry about the intellectual contribution of your professors. Even though intellectual contribution and academic publishing is the coin of the academic market, and it's what most of your workforce currently is chasing, it just doesn't move the needle. If you *are* going to try to tweak performance through intellectual contribution, you should steer faculty toward those 18 journals.

To really affect your Organizational Outcome, you need to make students and recruiters really happy with your school. The question is what you are willing and able to do to satisfy these customers that other business schools are not? For student satisfaction, you might achieve good scores through compelling teaching, but all your competitors are doing this too. Could you differentiate by building a strange workforce that truly pushes the MBA teaching envelope? Hire professors who skip the research since it's not important to winning anyway, and instead use their time networking with industry leaders who they can bring into the classroom? Maybe you could hire professors who really show students the love by inviting them over to their houses for picnics and volleyball, or meeting them out at the bars. This workforce might just be strange enough that other schools wouldn't imitate it and MBA students would view it as remarkable, giving you the highest marks on the *Business Week* survey.

What about the recruiter evaluations of your MBA program? How can you drive those numbers? You could produce well-trained grads who have the basics down cold and are confident but not pushy. Sounds just like what the competition is trying to do—good luck displacing schools ranked better than you with six times your endowment. What could you do that would be strangely and noticeably valuable? What if you got your faculty members to wine and dine company recruiters when they come in for interviewing? On one hand, it's blatant gaming because you're just creating interpersonal goodwill so that recruiters rate your school higher when they get surveyed by *Business Week*. On the other hand, professors might just learn what recruiters are looking for in MBA students that they aren't currently getting and then build this into their classes. For example, recruiters want more statistics and analytic ability from MBAs, and professors could add cases with datasets and make students run regressions and interpret output. Professors could make the cases and the classes compelling to MBAs by saying, "This is what Goldman Sachs told me they are looking for in job applicants." This could differentiate your school, and it would game your two most important metrics simultaneously. Sure, lots of professors wouldn't like the idea of using their personal time wining and dining recruiters; they might say that's not why they got a Ph.D. But what if you located and hired a strange breed of professor who liked hobnobbing with recruiters and building what they learned from recruiters into their classes?

In developing this example, I'm not actually suggesting that *Business Week* rankings provide a valid reflection of Business School success. For example, what would happen if *Business Week* suddenly increased the weight on intellectual contribution for ranking schools? What if *Business Week* loses relevance in ten years because the world really thinks universities should be judged by their intellectual contribution? Then your school could be in trouble because you built a strange schmoozing-type organization that was not equipped to contribute in intellectual ways. Listen, choosing a strategy is risky (it better be!), and my point here is not to suggest good versus bad strategies.

My point here is that if you want to know what your organization's Performance Drivers are, you need to first identity Organizational Outcome metrics that provide a valid reflection of what you think your organization exists to create. Then, literally find a way to make these metrics move in a way that your competitors are not willing or able to pursue. That's why we started with making sure your Organizational Outcomes were strategic and reflected what winning truly means to you. Once you choose Organizational

Outcomes and begin to take them seriously, they will affect everything you
do as an organization. They will affect what seems reasonable and what
seems valuable. In the MBA school example, if you as Dean had chosen a
slightly different metric—say the *U.S. News and World Report*'s rankings—
you would be placing your emphasis on MBA admissions because entering-
class GMAT scores drive this metric, but student and recruiter opinions are
not included in these rankings. Organizational Outcomes help expose and
pinpoint your Performance Drivers. By building an organization around gaming and measuring your Performance Drivers, you can build a strange, noticeable organization.

So here is what you need to do to figure out your own organization's
Performance Drivers:

1. Hold your Organizational Outcomes meeting, described in
    the last chapter. You and your top leadership team distill
    your strategy into three to four antagonistic metrics that let
    you know that you are winning in the way you want to
    win. Remember, each of your Organizational Outcomes
    must be a metric—actual numbers that you collect and
    store in a spreadsheet.

2. Soon after your Organizational Outcomes event, hold
    another meeting with the same group. This second meet-
    ing, or series of meetings, is going to be at least as long as
    the first one, probably much longer. The timing of this
    second meeting is important but difficult. You want to
    meet as soon as possible after the first one so that people
    still remember the Organizational Outcomes conversations
    and there is some momentum left. On the other hand, the
    second meeting can't be so soon that people are burnt out
    and frustrated and feel the need to "get back to their real
    work." They need to believe that this *is* their real work.
    These discussions and decisions will determine whether or
    not your organization wins over the next three years and
    whether it is still alive in ten.

3. For each of the Organizational Outcomes that you have
    developed, build consensus about three sets of questions:

    • What produces this Organizational Outcome number?
      Literally, what makes it go up or down?

- What are the two most important things our customers have to believe about us relative to our competition in order to affect this Organizational Outcome? How do we measure our progress toward creating these beliefs in our customers' heads?

- How can we influence this Organizational Outcome in a way that is valuable, rare, and hard to imitate? What are we willing and able to do that the competition is not in order to drive this Organization Outcome?

Let's dig deeper into these questions so that you know what you are looking for when you meet again as a leadership team.

Question 1: Producing the Result

- *What produces this Organizational Outcome number?*

- *Literally, what makes it go up or down?*

What you are looking to do here is theorize about the things that literally move your Organizational Outcome metrics. This is a brainstorming session about gaming the numbers you chose to represent winning. By gaming, I mean manipulating with the intent to change a specific outcome. Sometimes gaming creates value, and more often gaming destroys value. We are going to find a way to create value, meaning that you will not pursue all of the ideas that you discuss. The goal of this discussion is to think in far-reaching ways about what could move each Organizational Outcome causally, mechanically, and objectively.

The trick here: You need to let go of what you currently focus on and measure every day. Forgetting your existing approach may be harder than you think. Your minds and then your conversation will want to slip back to what you have been socialized to do ("the way we do things around here"). After a few hours, when you start wanting to wrap up the meeting up and get back to work, you will start formalizing "business as usual" without considering the full range of options. I'm sorry if this happens, because this will be your loss. The point here is not to simply formalize what you are already doing. The point is to deeply examine your current approach relative to the broader set of things you *could* be doing to game your Organizational Outcomes and add value to your customers in a unique way. You want to create a buffet of possible ways to affect your ultimate success, and then you want to screen the ideas to figure out which ones create long-term value.

So as a group, try to put your past assumptions about winning on hold for a while by just thinking objectively about your Organizational Outcome numbers and what makes them move. Sometimes it helps to get beyond the norms, illusions, and assumptions of insiders if you take the perspective of an outsider. This tactic can lead you down some dark alleys, but it also can reveal some conclusions that are both radical and rational. You want the meeting to take on a tone that allows people to say things like: "I'm not necessarily saying that we *should* do this, but if we *really* want to move that number, the way we could do it would be…"

Civil Engineers

Let's say your organization is a Stormwater Management Division of a civil engineering firm. Your primary client base consists of municipal clients with dedicated funding set aside to meet federal stormwater regulations. One of your primary Organizational Outcomes is year-over-year growth of business from existing clients. Based on client focus groups and your leadership team's discussion of why clients like your organization enough to issue new contracts, you believe that the most prominent Performance Driver of this outcome is meeting milestones and staying on schedule.

Now the fun begins because you need to take this concept—meeting project milestones—and convert it into a metric and a way of doing business that differentiates you from the competition on this dimension. The most obvious approach, your team decides, is to work closely with clients in the pre-project stage to create a realistic timeline of activities. Then the Performance Driver data can be the number of days after schedule the project teams complete the work. You've already been loosely tracking timetables anyway, and this is a nice chance to formalize the process into usable metrics. You decide to code completion as follows: A "0" means that you hit the target right on time; teams get an extra point for each day a stage is completed early; and teams get docked a point for each day a stage is missed.

This all seems pretty reasonable until someone on the leadership team says, "I'm not necessarily saying that we should do this…but if we really want to move that 'growth of existing business' number, we might want to focus on making clients *believe* that we hit the timeline targets, rather than measuring whether we *actually* hit the targets." He's not joking as some people initially thought. In fact, more discussion of this topic reveals that many times clients do not *want* work completed early because it throws off their schedules almost as badly as being late. OK, so no extra points for getting it done early. Fair enough. Then someone else says, "But other times, clients themselves build additional services into the project as it evolves, so that the original time table becomes sort of irrelevant." So we get clients to sign change orders when the schedule is renegotiated, and we use the new schedules to calculate the metric. Fair enough?

It turns out the very *best* project managers in your firm know how to take scheduling lemons and make them into lemonade by using scheduling issues to deepen the client relationship. What does this mean? It means that when they notice their teams falling behind schedule (bad weather, for instance), they personally call the client and talk about where things stand and how it looks like the timetable may be affected. They almost always are able to work out an agreement that everybody finds acceptable, and the two have a nice discussion about the Hockey Championship and the odds of Carolina taking the cup. In fact, the client is happier because of the call and the update than if the job had been done on time but with no personal update. This is how the best project managers drive future business.

This communication element of scheduling might actually be a differentiator for your organization. Although it sounds simple to maintain good client communication about project schedules, few engineering firms are willing to do what it takes to deliver on this dimension. The reality is that civil engineers often aren't. The personalities that gravitate toward an engineering career do not naturally lend themselves to maintaining good client rapport and communication. Most engineers by nature are somewhat introverted and tend to overanalyze problems. Introversion diminishes rapport probability while the tendency to overanalyze often leads to missed deadlines. So it would be a strange engineer (that is, a remarkably different breed of engineer) that you would need to hire and socialize in order to really win on this Performance Driver. You need engineers who actually *like* dealing with clients and who think creating and maintaining rapport and communicating about timelines is an important part of the job.

From this perspective, "meeting timeline targets" is not the best metric when it comes to gaming "growth of existing business." Maybe the right concept is "perceived responsiveness to scheduling and timetables," as rated by the client at the end of each project. You would need to build a very different mechanism for collecting and tracking this data. Your people would have to act in two very different way to affect these two different measures. Which is more reflective of your unique way of winning?

Question Set 2: Customer Beliefs

- *What are the one or two most important things our customers have to believe about us relative to our competition in order to affect this Organizational Outcome?*

- *How do we measure our progress toward creating these beliefs in our customers' heads?*

In most industries, you get to win because your customers say you win. They get to decide. So you need to get a handle on what would make them notice you, say nice things about you to their friends, and hand their money over to you. You may already have most of the answer to this question in your pocket because hopefully this emerged when you converted your story of winning into your Organizational Outcomes (see Chapter 3, "Organizational Outcomes: How Do I Know I Am Winning in the Way I Want to Win?"). The goal here is to formalize just what it is about your organization that customers are supposed to find so attractive and unique that you can count on them coming back for more. Then you need to build an organization around:

- Managing and gaming those customer perceptions

- Capturing some "upstream" data about those customer perceptions

Why do I say *one or two* most important things? The reason is to get you talking about *your most salient features*—or Performance Drivers—from the customer's perspective. Everything can't be prominent. There should be a very small number of very salient attributes that your target customers can lock in their heads about your organization. Sure, there are lots of "table stakes" that your organization delivers to customers, just like all the competition does. In the civil engineering organization, they need to be seen as credible and proficient engineers just like the competition, but the image of qualified engineers who deliver "good communication" and "timetable responsiveness" is remarkably out of the ordinary—it could be a differentiator.

> **There should be a very small number of very salient attributes that your target customers can lock in their heads about your organization.**

There are three reasons why it is so important to gather data about your Performance Drivers rather than just talking about them:

- **Most obvious**. Measuring Performance Driver data gives you a way to know if you are executing your unique strategy. It allows you to manage and not just hope.

- **Less obvious, but just as important**. The act of gathering Performance Driver data creates useful ripples throughout your organization. It shouts to employees (and you) what is very, very important. It affects how people think about their work and what identifies a valuable behavior. It makes you structure your organization in a way that maximizes your Organizational Outcomes.

- **Least obvious**. Trying to gather the right (valid) Performance Driver data helps you sharpen and clarify your competitive concepts. You get closer to your customers and gain better understanding of their needs and behaviors. As you translate strategic concepts into numbers that reflect reality, you continually learn more about the data, and you get more fine-grained in your classification of what is a win and what is a loss.

Back to School

Because these days all business schools are gaming the *Business Week* rankings, you as Dean decide to instead focus on what you believe is the true outcome of the business school: creating business leaders. You want to judge success based on the extent to which graduates of the programs do, in fact, assume leadership positions. Trying to develop an approach to capture standardized data on leadership has led to a lot of very useful questions about what exactly you mean by "creating leaders." For example: Could you quantify graduates' leadership success as position level in their firm with respect to the CEO? Or perhaps grads' leadership traits should be reported by their supervisors, subordinates, and peers? How long should it take for a graduate to "become" a leader—could each grad receive a score after ten years of work experience? Do you care about whether grads are leading in large, well-known firms (e.g., Wachovia) versus a small regional company or a family-run business? In the end, you figure out a way for each grad to receive a "leadership score" at two, five, ten, and fifteen years post-degree, and you also begin asking recruiters at your school about their perceptions of students' leadership potential.

The Leadership Scores become metrics your school starts to obsess about that most competitors aren't even tracking. The scores dictate your Performance Drivers and the type of organization you need to create in order to win. For example, to track information on graduates' leadership progression, you integrate the Office of Career Services with Alumni Affairs (these are separate in most schools). You decide that one of your Performance Drivers is "creating leadership opportunities" for students because in order to become better leaders, students need to try leading (which doesn't actually happen too much in classes). You begin to award faculty members raises and sometimes even tenure based on the number of leadership opportunities they establish with companies and oversee as project managers (other schools don't do this). You break entering students up into five-person project teams, and you develop a new curriculum structure where students alternate between a month of faculty instruction and a month of project execution within a partnership company (every other month one student leads the other four). Your school starts to look and feel radically different from the competition.

You also find that your obsession and investment into collecting data on your grads' leadership progress has some unintended, though very positive, consequences. For example, you find that

- The new program structure and the data about your graduates' leadership trajectories become selling tools for attracting both great students and great companies to recruit at your school.

- Keeping in touch with graduates to evaluate their leadership scores leads to more alumni donations to the school.

- Professors now keep in closer touch with their former students, which leads to more projects that future student teams can lead, more hiring of your MBA students into that organization, and more data for research.

- Alumni's enrollment in executive education programs increases, and you find for-fee service opportunities for the expanded Alumni-Career Services organization, such as ongoing leadership feedback and development programs.

You're not the Dean of a business school and my point here is not to encourage you to become one. My point is that you can stumbled on positive results when you obsess on creating, and measuring a salient image for your organization to deposit in customers' minds. This can lead to a very new type of customer experience with a different set of Performance Drivers based on gaming a different set of outcomes. The result is a new organizational focus that is valuable, rare, and difficult to imitate. Sure these changes will be risky—almost as risky as acting just like your competition—but you are starting to play the game your own way. You are starting to become strange.

Question Set 3: Deciding Which Game to Play

- *How can we influence this Organizational Outcome in a way that is valuable, rare, and hard to imitate?*

- *What are we willing and able to do that the competition is not in order to drive this Organizational Outcome?*

Hopefully, you and your leadership team will think up many viable ways to game each of your Organizational Outcome metrics. What you'll need then is a screen to sift the ideas through in order to determine which are worth pursuing and which need to be culled out. It's a little like panning for gold. Your culling discussion should revolve around the triumvirate of 1) value-creating; 2) rare; and 3) hard to imitate.

Value-creating means your approach to gaming the Organizational Outcome creates long-term usefulness, not short-term accomplishments that end up producing long-term destruction. In the Stormwater Management organization, a short-term accomplishment is cutting corners on installation quality to hit a project timetable. A long-term value creation is developing a deeper relationship with a client by calling and talking about priorities, progress, concerns, and sports. Both of these activities might affect clients' perceptions of your firm's ability to keep to a timetable, but one builds a future while the other destroys it.

Adding long-term value to customers is not enough because if your organization looks and feels to customers like the competition, then you are not developing a competitive advantage. What is your company willing and able to be known for in your customer eyes that your competitors aren't known for? How will you measure whether you have in fact become known for this unique element? This cuts to the heart of differentiating and establishing a competitive advantage.

What your organization is willing and able to do in terms of Performance Drivers determines the way your workforce must be strange (this is the focus of the next chapter). "Willing" means there is something that you and your workforce will suffer through to deliver long-term value to customers, while your competitors will not. It means that you are doing something both valuable and rare, and that, my friends, is a competitive advantage. "Able" means that there is something your workforce is uniquely qualified to do—some obsession, quality, or competency that allows them to deeply impress customers in a way that the competition could not do even if they were willing to try.

For example, say you own a small accounting firm that tracks repeat customer business as an Organizational Outcome, and you believe a key Performance Driver is customers' perceptions of your "accessibility." What are you willing and able to do to impress this accessibility image upon customers that your competitors are not? Are you willing and able to field customer's minor tax questions in real time when they call throughout the year? Are you willing and able to do this for free (if you can answer the question in less than 15 minutes)? Are you willing and able to hire and train someone to call each of your clients mid-year and gather their perceptions of your accessibility and service?

If you figure out Performance Drivers that your organization is willing and able to do that are valuable, rare, and hard to imitate, you can develop a sustainable competitive advantage. This your competitors simply cannot take from you even if they understand how you do it!)

Potential pitfall: Sometimes your discussion of this issue will make you realize that what it really takes to affect one of your Organization Outcomes are not things that you and the leadership team feel are best for your company, long-term. In other words, what your discussion may reveal is that you simply are NOT willing to do what it would take to game the metric. If this is the case, you probably have selected a wrong Organizational Outcome. Another way to say this is that you already "know" the answer of how you want to beat the competition and take their customers, and gaming this particular Organizational Outcome is not it. This is not a bad discovery—better now than after you have rolled out the wrong metrics throughout your organization and created workforce cynicism. But it does mean that you need to go back to Chapter 3 and redevelop your set of Organizational Outcomes so that you are measuring and focusing on the right things from the beginning.

Tears and Fears

The manager of a preschool serving two, three, and four year-olds believes that a key Performance Driver metric is "first day sticks." This does not refer to sticks and stones—it refers to the percentage of children who have a good first day experience at preschool and "stick" versus the percentage of meltdowns when parents can't bring themselves to pry their children from their legs or have to come pick up their children early because they won't stop crying. This is an extremely emotional time for many parents and children, since it often is the first major separation. It is symbolic and scary for both parties. It turns out that due to self-fulfilling prophecies, when the first day goes well, both parent and child feel strengthened and validated by the separation, and the rest of the week and the year are much more likely to be positive. When the first day ends in a tearful, fearful meltdown with an early parent pick-up, parents often pull their children from the class. Or, even if the child does remain enrolled, it causes trouble because the meltdown was rewarded and is more likely to reoccur, and the other children are upset by the meltdown. The next day the parents feel guilty and worried about the separation, which gives weird vibes to their children, which perpetuates the problem going forward.

What are the preschool teachers willing and able to do to game the metric of "first day sticks?" Two weeks before preschool starts, the teachers are willing to schedule one hour visits to each of the children's homes so that they initially meet them on their own turf. They are able to work with the children on decorating two pictures of an animal using special markers and glitter, and they have the parent take a photo of them with the child. This makes an early positive interaction and creates some familiarity with the teacher in a non-threatening situation that carries over to the first day. It also offers teachers early information about which kids are most fearful so that teachers can be prepared to give them extra support that first day. The photo and one animal picture is mailed back to the child (kids love to get mail, and the parents can put the pictures on the fridge). The teacher takes the other animal picture to school and tapes it to the front of the child's cubby so that when she or he sees it the first day, there is a connection between home and the school. The teachers schedule a second play date at the most fearful children's houses. Whenever the teachers see the kids with their parents out in the community, they mail a letter to the kids within two days telling them what a treat it was to see them again. After the first day of class, the teacher writes each parent a personalized email describing some activities the child did that day, along with "quiz questions" that parents can use to talk to their children about the first day (after the first day, the teachers tell the parents one or two things to ask about during the pickup). During the kids' first year, the teachers are willing to co-teach with the "next year" teacher a few times, so that the kids can start gaining familiarity and establishing comfort with their future teachers. The teachers likewise swap playground shifts so that the new teachers can have some fun with the kids and strengthen the initial bonds started during the co-teaching. They are willing to do all this in order to game first day sticks and get the school year started off right. Isn't that *strange*?

Linking It All Together

As you develop two to three Performance Drivers for each Organizational Outcome, you'll likely notice some trends. First, if you selected antagonistic Outcomes as we discussed in Chapter 3, you'll find that many of the games you might play to increase one Outcome only damages another. Accordingly, many Performance Drivers will have to be screened out, even though they would work great for a given Outcome.

You also may find a given Performance Driver that affects multiple Outcomes. For example, a business school Dean may find that when student teams participate in year-long leadership projects, they are more likely to respond positively to the *Business Week* survey, they are perceived as better leaders by companies, and they are more likely to donate to the school. Performance Drivers that affect multiple Organizational Outcomes in the right directions are gems and obviously should receive lots of attention and investment going forward.

Finally, you may find it useful to draw a picture—a causal map—of the linkages between Performance Drivers and Organizational Outcomes.[1] Graphic causal maps are useful because pictures are often more approachable than a spreadsheet and easier to walk other people through. Figure 4.2 shows a graphic approach you can use to "fill in the blanks" when you hold the Performance Driver meeting with your leadership team. Each oval represents a competitive construct (Reputation, for example), and the bullets within the circle represent the metrics or "proxies" that you have decided best reflect that concept (*Business Week* ranking, for example). You probably also will find it useful to capture some of the verbal logic your team develops to link each Performance Driver with each Outcome. If you use PowerPoint, this can be done by hyperlinking each arrow with a page of text that explains "how" the Performance Driver is linked to each Outcome. Getting down the logic you and your team created can be important because it may be hard to recreate the entire story later when some of the architects of the logic are no longer in the room.

---

[1]   For example, see Rucci, A. J., S. P. Kirn, & R. T. Quinn. "The Employee-Customer-Profit Chain at Sears," *Harvard Business Review*. January-February 1998 (#98109); Kaplan, R. S., & Norton, D. P. *Strategy Maps*. Boston: Harvard Business School Press, 2004.

A word of caution about causal maps: I have worked with companies that
had really polished-looking scorecards and causal maps of their strategies.
Unfortunately, nobody used them very much, and no data was being gathered
to manage to them or test them. Some fancy consulting firm had taken
their $150K and left them with a great-looking map of their strategy with
some "placeholder metrics" that no one actually believed in and no one was
actually gathering data on, and nothing had changed in the day-to-day operations. Do you remember that Billy Crystal skit on Saturday Night Live
where he said, "It's better to look good than to feel good?" I think that was a
joke, right?

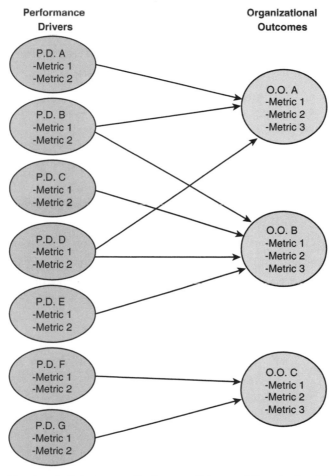

Figure 4.2   Mapping the links between Performance Drivers and Organizational Outcomes

All I'm saying here is be careful when you map out your strategy into a good-looking picture. Strategy maps have a way of packaging your messy work and making it all look very clean, neat, polished, and finalized. It often looks good even if it is not very good. Creating strategy pictures is useful but not nearly as useful as making sure of the following:

- That you have a clear story that you actually believe in that delineates what your organization creates that is valuable, rare, and hard to imitate.

- That you have worked really hard to translate this story into a set of competitiveness concepts that your organization is willing and able to do while other firms are not.

- That your leadership team agrees on the ways you are actually going to gather the data to represent your competitiveness concepts.

As long as you remember that a strategy picture is just some pretty wrapping and is not the solution itself, you should be fine.

Where Do We Go from Here?

Now you have the tools to determine what you need to offer to your target customers in order to stand out and take them and their money from your competitors. *Next stop:* How must your workforce be remarkably out of the ordinary, unusual, and striking in order to achieve your Performance Drivers? What does your strange workforce need to deliver to make the strategy come to life?

5

Strange Workforce Deliverables: What Our Workforce Does to Make Customers Notice and Love Us

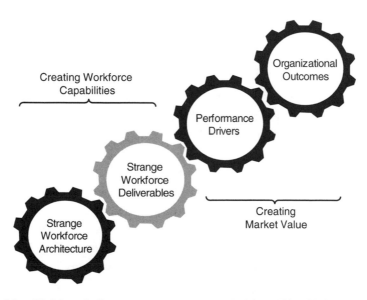

Figure 5.1   Workforce Deliverables and your Strange Workforce Value Chain

The whole point of this book is to help you build a strange workforce. So why the heck did it take five chapters to get here? Because it is not enough to be just any old type of strange. For instance, if your workforce is strange in ways that customers don't care about, it won't work. Or if your workforce is strange in a way that customers like, but it costs too much to be that strange, it won't work. Strange must be disciplined and developed into what

> **Strange must be disciplined and developed into what it takes to impress customers and leave competitors behind in a sustainable way.**

it takes to impress customers and leave competitors behind in a sustainable way. With you as the conductor, strange must be orchestrated so that it results in an affordable symphony that your customers love to come and listen to.

Look at Figure 5.1. What we have done so far in the book is figure out what type of symphony is compelling to your target audience. In other words, the first two stages of our Value Chain focused on what your organization does to create market value and how you go about measuring it. We started not with the means (your workforce) but the end in mind. So we started with the proof that you were winning in your unique way, and then we moved to what your organization must create to make customers notice and love you. Together these two steps give a definite direction to the particular type of strange you need. The competitive concepts and metrics that spring from Chapters 3 and 4 help you understand how your workforce must be strange in order to create market value.

Now look at the figure again. Creating market value depends on—literally pivots on—your workforce's capabilities. Your strategy for creating market

> **Your strategy for creating market value is just a bunch of ideas until some people in your organization make those ideas happen.**

value is just a bunch of ideas until some people in your organization make those ideas happen. It's not that strategy is hooey—if you are going to win, you need to be right in your ideas of what customers want. However, even if your ideas about what customers want are right, they just sit there as ideas that customers don't notice until your workforce enacts them.

"Workforce capabilities" may sound like a mouthful, but it really just means what your people are strangely good at doing. If you are a sole proprietor and you are your only employee, then off you go to personally do all of the strange things that will make customers notice your organization and want to give you their money. If you lead an organization of employees, then you as conductor need to figure out exactly who has to act strange in what ways and at what times to make your Performance Drivers happen. What unique experience will customers have when they interact with your organization that they do not experience with the competition, and how does your workforce make this unique experience occur? That is what we're doing in this chapter. We're going to figure out exactly how your workforce must be strange and what they need to obsess about, in order to make you win.

Play Your Own Game[1]

With the second-lowest payroll in baseball, the Oakland Athletics were not going to get into the playoffs or win the World Series playing the same game as the other teams who had three to four times their payroll. They needed to develop their own way of winning, and they needed to build a strange workforce to translate that strategy into a reality.

The Oakland A's approach to winning baseball was accomplished by re-thinking how winning is accomplished. According to the A's, the Organizational Outcome is to win games, and you win games when players don't make outs. Because three outs define an inning, anything that increases the offense's chances of making an out is bad, and anything that decreases outs is good. Based on this logic, a key Performance Driver of winning games was on-base percentage because it is the best reflection of whether or not a batter will be a step toward winning or the end of winning.

The general manager, Billy Beane, was a former player who experienced first-hand how traditional baseball scouts undervalued on-base percentage. From his perspective on winning, scouts overvalued the wrong player attributes (e.g., physical build and attractiveness, footspeed, fielding ability),

---

[1]   This chapter borrows heavily from the wonderful book: Lewis, M. 2003. *Moneyball: The Art of Winning an Unfair Game.* New York: W. W. Norton & Co. You really need to read it if you have not already.

overvalued the wrong player statistics (e.g., stolen bases, RBIs), and overvalued the wrong sources for talent (high school teams) when building baseball teams. This means that if the Oakland A's could be disciplined enough to ignore traditional assumptions about baseball and baseball players, they could build a strange, valuable workforce on the cheap.

In contrast to the traditional baseball model that celebrated aggressive swinging and deemed players selfish if they drew a walk with a guy on second, the Oakland A's wanted *thoughtful hitters* who swung at what they could hit and let the rest go as balls. The Oakland A's obsession with on-base percentage as their Performance Driver resulted in a very strange team. For example, this obsession made Billy Beane want to hire Steve Stanley, who was a center fielder from Notre Dame. Despite Stanley's proven knack for getting on base better than almost anyone else, the traditional scouts from the other teams believed Stanley was not big enough to play (5'7" and 155 pounds), and therefore he was hugely undervalued when the A's approached him. Stanley himself did not expect to be drafted until the fifteenth round—that is, basically he expected to be hired to fill out some team's minor league roster. The A's, based on their strange model of winning, offered Stanley a second-round draft pick if he would sign at about $500,000 less than every other second-round pick. He did.

Other teams assumed that the A's signed people like Stanley because they couldn't afford anyone else. But the interesting truth is that Billy Beane wanted to sign people like Stanley far more than many of the expensive players that the competition was outbidding itself to hire. The A's found a deliverable and a metric that a very strange workforce could exploit to win baseball games. The beauty of the metric is that the competition didn't even care about it, creating the undervaluation that gave the A's their competitive advantage. Based on a Performance Driver metric that other teams did not value, the A's approached players who expect to get drafted in the nineteenth round, offered hundreds of thousands of dollars less than they were "worth" (to the A's, that is) and got twice the team commitment. These players' strange skills had been undervalued all their baseball lives so that even though Jeremy Brown had the best offensive record the University of Alabama had ever seen from the A's perspective, it was hard for him to believe that a major league team would even be interested in him. The average big league salary was $2.3 million, and the average A's opening day salary was less than $1.5 million.

When you obsess about on-base percentage, and you hire enough people who exemplify on-base percentage every day, your organization starts to take on a strange culture relative to other baseball teams. Different norms of what is right and wrong develop. To maximize the A's on-base percentage, for example, every batter needed to behave like a leadoff man at the plate with the goal of getting on base. Bunts and sacrifice flies to advance other runners became scorned. Swinging for bad pitches was viewed as an unacceptable, destructive addiction, while a willingness to take a base on balls was virtuous. Stealing bases became regarded as dumb and selfish because it threatened the goal of avoiding outs. What was built was a strange-looking, strange-acting team that was less likely to produce outs than the competition, which led to more wins.

Billy's first year on the job with the Oakland A's was 1998, when the team went 74–88. In 1999, the A's finished 87–75 and missed the playoffs. In 2000, the A's won 91 games, and in 2001 they won 102 games, and made the playoffs both years. These were years when the *gap* between the Yankees' and the A's opening day payrolls went from $62 million in 1999 to $90 million in 2002. In 2002, the A's won 103 games in the regular season and took the record for most games won in a row (20).

But That's Just Baseball, Right?

Is it really possible that you could find these types of inefficiencies in your *own* market? Is it really possible that there is a special breed of person out there who is predestined to make your strategy go but who is paradoxically undervalued by the market? Consider two perspectives:

- A strange workforce that delivers what your customers like but your competitors think is dumb means that, by definition, your competition will undervalue the people you need the most. When you try to win in a strange way, it means competitors aren't trying to win that way, which then means they aren't valuing the strange workforce traits that you are. And this means you can create a competitive advantage "buying strange" on the cheap and then selling results to the marketplace in a way your competitors aren't willing or able. But if you play the game just like all your competitors, then you will basically all be trying to hire the same people with the same characteristics. If this is the case, then there may not be any great values out there for you, and customers probably won't notice anything extraordinary about your organization.

- Market inefficiencies develop out of poor measurement. Even if you are trying to beat your competitors at their own game, you can locate and capture market inefficiencies if you are able to define and measure performance better than your competitors. You literally can see value that they do not see. "If gross miscalculations of a person's value could occur on a baseball field, before a live audience of 30,000 and a television audience of millions more, what did that say about the measurement in other lines of work? If professional baseball players could be under- or over-valued, who couldn't?"[2] Most organizations don't do a great job of measuring performance because measuring the right things in a valid way is very hard. You don't want to be like other organizations. You want to be strange.

Your job as a leader is to figure out what strange obsession your workforce should have in order to maximize wins, and then you need to find a valid way to measure it and make it happen.

You may not be able to get workers at half price like Billy Beane did, but here is the message to you, one more time: Your job as a leader is to figure out what strange obsession your workforce should have in order to maximize wins, and then you need to find a valid way to measure it and make it happen.

Hot Dog!

Did you ever watch a hot dog eating contest? Usually the winners are people who elevate hotdog eating to an art form—it's not even about hot dogs anymore. It's about executing a process that has been perfected through devotion. It's usually not the largest person with the biggest belly that wins. It's

---

[2] Moneyball, p. 72.

the person who executes a process like a machine. When you watch it, the devotion to the craft is sort of unparalleled. It's so starkly amazing that anyone would be so devoted to this particular activity that it sort of inspires awe. "That dude is strange," you say, but you also find yourself impressed and intrigued. And you sure as hell find yourself unwilling to imitate it.

What is your organization's hot dog-eating event? What strange activity is it that you and your workforce have mastered better than anyone else? What can you create in your market that inspires incredulity, in both your customers and your competitors? I worked with a telecommunications tower company that was absolutely obsessed with the time it took to get a new customer up and running and functional using their technology. The industry average was three days, and they were more like 22 hours. They talked about it all the time; everything touching this "up-time process" became practiced, rehearsed, and greased. When you signed on as a customer, people almost killed themselves to get you connected up *yesterday*. It would make you shake your head and wonder about them a little. But at the same time, this was something customers cared a lot about, and the strange devotion created a strong initial positive impression of the company that lasted. It was something that customers told friends about.

Make sure you find some value-creating activity that your workforce elevates to an art form. What will you will obsess about and practice and get down so pat that you become mercenary in your execution? Picture the hot dog-eating champion. Have Carly Simon's "Nobody Does It Better" playing as background music. I think you pretty much get the message here.

Building Strange Means "Good" People Will Quit

If you establish new metrics that symbolize success and change the way the game is played in your organization, you need to be prepared to lose some of your "best" employees. Here's why:

When you forge a strange new definition of winning, it creates new demands for how your workforce must act. Some of your best people will be willing and able to adapt their skills toward your strange approach to business, and will be invigorated by the new way of winning. Others will not be willing, or able, to start playing according to your new rules. Remember, you have designed your version of strange to be hard to imitate. By design, it will not be easy for normal contributors to change to strange. After Billy Beane started building his strange workforce based on proven on-base percentage rather than foot speed and player attractiveness, most of the existing scouts left the A's at the end of the season to get jobs with other teams that cared more about their expertise. What they were best at Billy didn't care for.

The people who are best at winning the normal way become undervalued by your organization once you change to strange. This process is the mirror image of how the strange people you need most are undervalued by the normal market. People who have a great talent conducting "business as normal" will no longer be treated like they are great at your organization. It's nothing personal—it's just that their "traditional" skills will not help you win your own way. This means that your best people who are superior at conducting business as normal can get a better deal at normal organizations. You have intentionally created a situation where the market now values normal skill sets more than you do.

Example: When Ray Durham was with the Oakland A's, he felt like a fish out of water.[3] He was bred on being aggressive running and stealing bases. Other teams he played on never dreamed of being passive about base-running and stealing bases. The White Sox had always told him that an aggressive mistake was not really a mistake. Staying put on base and not taking running risks was simply an unnatural act to Ray—it was like not breathing. This specimen who had perfected the art of base-running found that at the A's, no one *cared* about it. The same phenomenon will happen in your organization when your new strange rules take people who are natural stars in the normal game and devalue the very traits that made them great.

On the other hand, when you have people who are strange in ways that are needed most by your strategy to make your Performance Drivers move, they experience a deeply satisfying reward that money cannot buy. Case in point: Scott Hatteberg was a thoughtful hitter who was strange in his patience in waiting for his pitches, getting on base, and not striking out.[4] In 2002, he was thirteenth in the American League in on-base percentage, and he was

[3] Moneyball, p. 266–268.

[4] Moneyball, p. 177–179.

fourth in the American League in his ratio of walks-to-strikeouts. He was a champ at wearing out pitchers and exposing their best pitches to the rest of the team. In 2002, he finished third in the league in pitches-seen-per-plate-appearance. Hatteberg was not a good fit with the Red Sox, where they ostracized hitters who did not exhibit aggressiveness at the plate, and they called you selfish if you walked with a guy on second base. If Hattenberg let a pitch go by that he couldn't do much with, Red Sox managers would holler at him, coaches would tell him he was hurting the team, and he was ridiculed in front of other players by the hitting coach. Each time Hatteberg came to bat, he had to take an "intellectual stand against his own organization"[5] to do what he did best. Nobody at the Red Sox suggested there was anything valuable about his approach to working the count, drawing walks, getting on base, and not making outs. From the first day he started with the Oakland A's, much of the misery in his career evaporated. "Here I go 0 for 3 with two lineouts and a walk, and the *general manager* comes by my locker and says, 'Hey, great at bats.'"[6] For the first time in his career, other players told Hatteberg they liked his approach, and managers encouraged his strange innate style. Hatteberg's response was, "This is the most fun I've had since Triple-A."[7] When you find people with strange personal characteristics that match your strategy and its strange needs, those people get to operate day-in and day-out in an environment that celebrates and rewards their strengths. It is reassuring and comfortable and hard to think about leaving, even for more money.

When some of your "best" employees go to other firms, lots of people (including the new firm who picked them off) won't be able to believe that you let them go so easily. People will laugh and scoff. But according to your new metrics, these individuals are no longer as valuable to you as they are to the normal market. These people have two good reasons to leave: They won't like performing in your strange situation psychologically, and they will be better off financially if they leave because the market values their normal skills more than you do. Can you get inner peace knowing you are right when lots of people are saying you're wrong? Can you smile when two of your "best" people (according to the normal standard) get picked off by

[5]   Moneyball, p. 179.

[6]   Moneyball, p. 179.

[7]   Moneyball, p. 179.

competitors who value them more? Can you say convincingly to yourself and others, "They will be a better fit there—they are not strange like us." Can you use the hole they create as an opportunity to promote people within your organization that personify the new strange? The journey to strange is not for the weak of heart; it's for leaders who want to win pretty badly.

Strange Workforce Deliverables: Workforce-Wide Versus Job-Specific

The phrase "Strange Workforce Deliverables" sort of makes it sound like the entire lot of people in your organization need to be strange in the same way—as if all your employees, workforce-wide, need to have some innate quirk that makes them stand out as particularly valuable to you and your strategy. As if once upon a time a strange tribe existed and somehow got blown apart and dispersed throughout the world, and your job as a leader is to find these people and reassemble them back as a tribe right there in your organization.

But even more often, the meaning of the phrase "Strange Workforce Deliverables" depends on what particular job you're talking about. In other words, what an employee needs to obsess about to move your Performance Drivers depends on the role that the employee plays in creating value within the organization. To make your organization stand out to customers, your salespeople and engineers might need to be strange in some of the same ways, but they might also need to be strange in some very different ways.

For the rest of this chapter, we're going focus on the idea of workforce-wide deliverables. In the next chapter, we will deal with the topic of job-specific strange deliverables and find ways to make sure you deliver strange to your customers one job at a time.

Workforce-Wide Strange Deliverables

What obsession does everybody in your organization need to bring to the party to make your organization stand out? Lots of firms think that they have the answer to this question, and they call them "core values" or sometimes "core competencies." They usually have about eight of them, and they usually include teamwork, integrity, initiative, and accountability. And excellence, don't forget excellence. If this sounds like your list, then you are in very good company.

The first problem is that this is not a place where you want to be in good company. These certainly are nice, useful traits to have in a workforce, in the same way that electricity is useful to have. But will this generic list differentiate you in customers' eyes? Can these workforce traits make you strangely valuable to the market if every other organization, including your competition, is trying to build them into their workforces too?

The second problem is that these workforce characteristics probably are not tightly linked to your Performance Driver metrics, because vague workforce traits like "initiative" are not the best way to game your unique Performance Drivers. Think deterministically about Performance Drivers: What makes them go up and down? Try to think of your Workforce Deliverables as gears in an engine that need to line up almost perfectly with your Performance Driver gears (like Figure 5.1), so that when your Workforce Deliverables turn, it makes it very likely than the Performance Drivers turn. Your job as leader is to minimize the slippage that occurs between these gears. Remember, workforces are means to achieving your organization's ends.

Does your organization need any workforce-wide characteristics that are unique to your strategy? I think I hear another call for a leadership team meeting, with the same cast of characters as the last two meetings. Try to time this third meeting close enough to the Performance Drivers meeting that people remember the previous conversations and there is still some momentum. You want the feel of the meeting to be "work in progress," not "revisiting ancient history" or "*so* last year."

Prior to the meeting, draw your causal strategy map on a big white board in the front of the room or hand them out. Put something together so that before you get started, everyone can see each of your Performance Driver concepts and metrics and can see how your Performance Drivers affect each of your Organizational Outcomes (see Figure 4.2). Then, for each Performance Driver, you and your leadership team need to build consensus around three sets of questions:

- To make our Performance Drivers move, how must our workforce be distinct from our competitors? What characteristics describe our ideal workforce that our competitors would not or could not use to describe their workforces?

- Where are the gears currently slipping? What characteristics of our existing workforce must change in order for us to execute our strategy?

- How can we measure our Strange Workforce Deliverables rather than just talking about them? How do we go from workforce concepts to workforce metrics?

Let's unpack these questions so you know what you're fishing for in your leadership discussion.

Question Set 1: Distinctiveness

- *To make our Performance Drivers move, how must our workforce be distinct from our competitors?*

- *What characteristics describe our ideal workforce that our competitors would not or could not use to describe their workforces?*

The point of these questions is to get away from talking about nice, pleasant, plain-vanilla workforce characteristics and start focusing on any strange, differentiating characteristics that actually can move your unique Performance Drivers. Your goal is to find a way for your organization to take risks that you think are intelligent, your customers value, and that your competitors will not or cannot pursue. Southwest Air associates and pilots like to have fun at work. They wear those short pants and Hawaiian shirts, they joke around and have fun with passengers, the pilots help load the luggage on the plane if the departure is late...and this just is not how most airlines see the world. It is much more important for most airline associates to follow rules and procedures than it is to connect interpersonally with passengers. Most airlines' workforces see a barrier between the baggage handler and pilot that is never to be crossed, a sort of social caste system. They see joking and short pants as opposite the way pilots are *supposed* to look and act, which is serious, stately, and almost military in disposition. It probably would not seem natural for normal Continental Pilots to load bags, wear floral shirts to work, or joke with passengers—it isn't something that they want to do. So when

Continental tried imitating the Southwest approach (Continental Lite), the experiment failed quickly.[8]

Harley Davidson might want employees to be Bikers and Harley owners before they become employees. Everyone from designers to materials managers to salespeople to maintenance staff should own and love a Harley and be able to talk about their relationship with motorcycles. Being associated with Harley Davidson should not be something they do just for a paycheck. In order to build the brand loyalty and maintain street credibility, they should honestly love (and maybe even live for) the open road on a motorbike, and be passionate about the freedom symbolized by a Harley. If one of your Performance Drivers is maintaining close contact with Harley owners, how do you connect closely with that strange tribe unless you are one of the tribe? If you want to offer innovations in bikes and accessories that Harley owners find compelling, then you need to have design people that want it themselves when they are riding and hear about it from other Bikers when they are out riding and talking. If you want credibility in your sales force, and they don't have a yearning to be out there with two wheels and the open road under their feet, making people look when the engine crackles with that Harley roar, then you have impostors that fail to build rapport with real Harley owners. Sure, it is also nice if they value initiative and accountability, but if they don't see being a Harley Biker as a lifestyle choice—as a major chunk of their identity—then they can go work at some other place that manufactures and sells motorized equipment.

Question Set 2: Strange Changes

- *Where are the gears currently slipping?*

- *What characteristics of our existing workforce must change in order for us to execute our strategy?*

Many organizations are trying to execute a strategy with a workforce that was created to solve different types of problems that existed in the past. Does your current workforce, which you mostly inherited, have the necessary strange

---

[8] O'Reilly, C., & Pfeffer, J. *Southwest Airlines: Using Human Resources for Competitive Advantage.* Harvard Business School. HR1A.

> **Many organizations are trying to execute a strategy with a workforce that was created to solve different types of problems that existed in the past.**

behaviors and characteristics that it will take to make your current strategy go? If there is slippage between your workforce characteristics and your Performance Drivers, this is a common problem and is nothing to be ashamed of. But you can't get your strategy executed until you fix it. You either need to change the strategy or change the way the workforce acts.

As the leader of a wealth management organization in a large bank, your change strategy is to focus on high-wealth ($5 million to $100 million net worth) individuals so you can produce higher profits with fewer client interactions and fewer consultants. However, most of your existing consultants have built nice, solid businesses with net worth clients in the $500K to $900K range. They are good, hard workers, but something is starting to slip between the workforce and your new strategy because this lower range is the wealth level where many of your consultants are comfortable talking to clients, where they personally share many of clients' own needs and values, and where their understanding of wealth management products is most pronounced. Most of your existing workforce will be intimidated by "going out for big bear" both because it is uncomfortable to leave a strategy that has treated them well throughout their careers and because they personally have far less in common with the higher wealth society. What do they like to talk about? What do they think is important? What wealth management vehicles are best positioned to meet their needs? A Strange Workforce Deliverable that might serve this organization are "high society" network connections and background so that your consultants have a comfort level talking with and creating relationships with the $10 million to $100M net worth crowd.

It may sound like common sense that you would need to match up your workforce's unique traits with your Performance Drivers, as you sit there and read about it in this book. But if it's common sense, it sure isn't very common. More often, firms change the strategy but not the workforce. What are the odds of that working? To make it happen, you need to take the uniqueness of your Performance Drivers very seriously and think new thoughts about how you need to change your workforce to move your Performance Drivers. Then you have to translate your fuzzy workforce concepts (like interpersonal comfort with high-wealth clients) into something you can measure and use to manage your workforce. Developing measures will put teeth into your management of the concepts and also will ensure that the leadership team agrees about what the concepts even mean. Then the metrics become a way to make the organization obsess about the right customers and the right outcomes, based on the strategy (and not based on "the comfortable way we have always done it."). Some of your "best" wealth management consultants will get angry and insulted when you try to refocus them on bigger game clients. Some of them will go to the competition, taking some of their "best" clients with them, and your competition will laugh at how easily you let them go. You have to believe in your strategy and your Strange Workforce Deliverables enough if you want to be confident that both you and your departed employees are better off by the separation.

All you need to do is remember that the Performance Drivers will not happen magically. They will only happen if customers notice something distinctive and valuable about your organization. If there is something special in your workforce that needs to be there to turn your Performance Driver gears, and that special something isn't there, the gears won't drive. At this point in the book, don't worry about *how* to fix the gaps you expose in your workforce. That is the goal of Chapters 7 through 9. That's where we can figure out how to set up a system that gets you the right workforce to execute your strategy. For now, be objective and isolate any slippage that exists between your Workforce Deliverable gears and your Performance Driver gears.

Question Set 3: Measurement and Metrics

- *How can we measure our Strange Workforce Deliverables rather than just talking about them?*

- *How do we go from strange workforce concepts to strange workforce metrics?*

So far in this third meeting, you've been talking about workforce concepts. You and your leadership team have talked about and identified one or two strange workforce characteristics needed to make your Performance Drivers turn and your strategy go. Here's a little quiz: Talk is cheap and easy. Measuring is valuable but difficult. Which has a better chance at giving you a competitive advantage? To bring your words and concepts down to earth and make them usable, we need to figure out a way to measure them.

How can you measure the Strange Workforce Deliverables that you need to execute your strategy? Here are two things to push you in the right direction. First, if you have not read Chapter 10 yet ("The Magic of Metrics: Creating and Implementing Measurement Systems"), this might be the perfect time to read that and think about how to quantify your own concepts. Second, here is a set of discussion questions that help leaders who want to take Workforce Deliverables more seriously than their competitors. For each Workforce Deliverable (for example, some basic trait, value, or competency you and the leadership team agree everyone should possess), ask yourselves:

- How do we prove that one job applicant or employee brings us the strange deliverable while another job applicant or employee does not?

- How does this workforce concept reveal itself in actual behaviors or results that customers will notice and care about?

- What evidence of the strange deliverable could we witness in the real world?

- How can we build a process to gather data on this phenomenon?

If Harley cares about the "biker status" of employees, they could measure the number of years each employee (and job seeker) has owned a Harley and then track the workforce average, minimum, and maximum. They could cut the data by function or job level. They could ask for photo support—it could be fun, but they could take it seriously.

If Home Depot cares about contractor-grade skills, they could give timed simulation tests in plumbing, wiring, and masonry. Each employee could get a score upon hire and then upon each anniversary, and Home Depot could track the workforce average, minimum, and maximum, and likewise cut the data by function, or job level, or peak store times.

If "sports and fitness obsession" were important to Nike's workforce, they could measure each job seekers' favorite athletic event and personal best in that event. They could have another employee who is serious at that event compete with them and verify their intensity and ability. They could rate the ability percentage of each employee relative to the national norms. They could have employees report the number of times they work out each week. Nike could track the workforce average, minimum, and maximum, and cut the data by function, or job level.

Do you think these measurement approaches would put some teeth into the concepts and make these companies more strange along these dimensions? Yep, job seekers and employees would probably notice these initiatives. Think that it sounds like a lot of effort and work? Yep. Would you prefer to just talk about strange workforce concepts, or do you actually want to make something noticeable happen in your organization? This is an example of a place where you need to find the good pain: What is so important and distinctive about your workforce that is worth a lot of pain to get activated?

Possible Hope for Winning Through Generic Workforce Characteristics

Let's say your leadership team completes this meeting and what you have revealed is that your workforce deliverables *just aren't very strange*. What you need from your workforce *really are* the same traits as most other organizations (teamwork, accountability, and the like). Well, it's not a good sign, and it's going to be harder to differentiate your organization. However, there is still one way you can distance your organization from the competition using the same list of generic workforce characteristics as your competitors. How? By taking the concepts more seriously and by putting sharper teeth into them.

To beat competitors at their own game, it helps to be way more serious about the game than they are. You need to be able to define and measure how those generic core values and competencies really manifest themselves in your organization. Develop better measurement of the workforce characteristics than your competitors. If you obsess on achieving these workforce characteristics and develop them into an art form, then guess what—you are strange and hard to imitate! To get there, you need to be able to answer the question, "What do we measure to demonstrate that we have pushed these common workforce characteristics far enough so that customers notice a difference in what our workforce delivers?" With better measurement, you have better information to beat the market. You can locate the necessary workforce traits more effectively than your competition, making it more likely that you can out-execute them on a daily basis.

The Catch

When you take this measurement task seriously—for example, when you honestly try to determine what you mean by "teamwork" and how you would measure the extent to which a given employee is or is not exhibiting teamwork—you will usually find that it depends on the particular job. Teamwork means something different to a salesperson than to an internal auditor, and teamwork manifests itself in very different behaviors across job types. To get the level of specificity that you need to measure the workforce characteristics better than your competitors, you need to dig into what this means, day to day, to actual employees. Almost always, this exercise reveals that the operational definition of your workforce deliverables depends on which particular job type you are referring to. This brings us to job-specific deliverables, which is the topic of the next chapter.

6

Job-Specific Strangeness: Different Deliverables from Different Jobs

Figure 6.1   Workforce Deliverables and your Strange Workforce Value Chain

Let Me Guess...

You read the last chapter. You and your leadership team met to figure out what strange workforce characteristics your entire workforce needs to deliver. But…all the characteristics you came up with depended on which job you were discussing. For example, you definitely were able to isolate some strange characteristics that your salespeople should possess that the competitors would not be willing or able to copy. But these were different from the strange characteristics you need your Research and Development people to have.

If you can't find any strange deliverables that are needed across your entire workforce, it's OK. Relax. I call this the "myth of core competencies." I know that workforce core competencies are in vogue right now and that organizations are supposed to find traits that everyone from the janitor to the CEO needs to demonstrate. But let's be realistic: Very often there is not a single set of traits that everyone in your workforce needs in order to be distinctive to the customer and beat the competition. Sure, the notion of a set of core competencies that applies across all employees sounds simple and clean, and it would make hiring and performance appraisals easier. I want simple too, when it is also correct. But in reality, what it takes to move your Performance Drivers often is a bunch of different deliverables from different jobs that complement each other rather than duplicate each other. It's more like a puzzle where each job's deliverables need to fit together to form a cohesive whole that makes customers say, "Wow!"

For example, a wood shipping company is trying to differentiate from competitors by having truck drivers do the following:

- Learn the names of the plant managers on their routes.

- Build in extra time to arrive early, spend some time hanging around the plant, and talk with the plant manager on duty.

- Take a walk around the plant and see how the current stock looks and take notes on whether the plant might make an "emergency rush order" later that month.

- Type this information into a database that the whole company can access.

These are strange Workforce Deliverables (ordinary truck drivers just don't normally perform these services), but these deliverables don't apply to the company's loaders or accountants.

Sure, the loaders and accountants need to be good employees, but here are two important issues that cannot be overlooked. First, getting the strange deliverables from the truck drivers is *more important* to making customers notice, and executing the company's strategy, than the deliverables of the loaders and the accountants. Second, the loaders and the accountants do not need to be strange *in the same way* the truck drivers do. So both the *importance* and the *meaning* of strange depends on which job we're talking about.

What about the jobs in your company? How can you decide about the importance and the meaning of strange for your jobs? Sounds like it's time to have another meeting—or series of meetings, actually. So far, we have been dealing with your organization as a whole. We have worked through your Organizational Outcomes, Performance Drivers, and Workforce-wide Deliverables in a way that encompasses your entire organization. Now, for job-specific Workforce Deliverables, we need to walk through each of the jobs in your organization separately. What makes your job-specific deliverables strange and effective depends on why the job exists in your organization, and the only way to figure this out is to work through each job, one at a time. Will these job-specific discussions be time-consuming? Yes, they will be—and painful to boot. Using the exercise analogy, these are the painful repetitions that will make you stronger. This is exactly why most of your competitors are messing this up and not executing their strategies and why most consumers don't notice much difference between organizations. You have to want to win pretty bad to get this deep into the process of winning, and most leaders aren't this deep into the process.

For each job in the organization you lead, here are the questions you need to be able to answer:

- How much strategic leverage does this job have? Is this job an *executor*, an *operator*, or an *outsourcer*? How much does good versus bad performance on this job affect whether we differentiate our organization and execute our strategy?

- Why can't we just outsource this job? What Performance Drivers does this job affect?

92 CHANGE TO STRANGE

- What does strange look like for this job based on our strategy? What are the characteristics of people in this job that differentiate our organization from a customer perspective?

- How do I measure the Workforce Deliverables for this job, rather than just talking about them? How would I distinguish the best employee I have from the worst in terms of what they accomplish, how they act, and what they know?

Let's dig into each of these questions a little more.

Question Set 1: Job Leverage

- *How much strategic leverage does this job have? Is this job an* **executor**, *an* **operator**, *or an* **outsourcer**?

- *How much does good versus bad performance on this job affect whether we differentiate our organization and execute our strategy?*

All jobs are not created equal. Nothing personal, but some jobs are more important to executing your strategy than other jobs.[1] You already know this in your heart, of course. But it is currently not in vogue to say it out loud or do anything about it. Most companies want to treat all employees as if they are somehow equally important, all unique flowers to be cultivated equally. Because of this, most companies are unwilling to be very strategic about how

> **Nothing personal, but some jobs are more important to executing your strategy than other jobs.**

they treat different jobs depending on the linkage between the job and their Performance Drivers. You can use this to your advantage. You do not want to be like other organizations. You want to build a strange organization.

---

[1] Huselid, M. A., R. W. Beatty, and B. E. Becker. "'A Players' or 'A Positions?' The Strategic Logic of Workforce Management," *Harvard Business Review,* 2005: Reprint R0512G; Boudreau, J. and P. M. Ramstad. "Where's Your Pivotal Talent?," *Harvard Business Review,* 2005: Reprint F0504K.

For the wood shipping company described earlier, an important component of the company's strategy for differentiating and winning rests on the shoulders of the truck drivers because two of the Performance Drivers are

- Plant managers' perceived trust and communication with the company

- Percentage of emergency loads shipped within 24 hours at "crisis prices."

These Performance Drivers don't happen magically. They happen when individual truck drivers build solid interpersonal relationships with plant managers and gather warehouse inventory information. These actions are valuable, rare, and reasonably difficult to imitate because it takes a strange truck driver to be willing and able to do these activities and to think these activities are an important part of the job and perhaps even enjoyable. This is an *executor* job in this company because truck drivers bear a very heavy responsibility for, differentiating the company in customers' eyes, and making the Performance Drivers move. The truck drivers are emissaries and visible manifestations of the shipping company, and they can make the company remarkable and out of the ordinary from a customer perspective. If executors fail, strategy dies. The shipping company should be willing to invest an enormous amount of energy making sure its truck drivers are strange, including how the company goes about identifying and hiring strange truck drivers, how much they are willing to pay for these strange employees, and how they socialize and train them to make sure they start and stay strange. If you really want your Performance Drivers to move, shower the most attention and investment on the people who execute your company's strategy, not the people highest in the organizational chart, not the people who have been there the longest, and not the people with the sexiest job titles.

> **If executors fail, strategy dies.**

This shipping company also has loaders who package the wood bundles and operate forklifts to load the trucks. Loaders are integral to the operations of the company because trucks need to be loaded on time to get to the customers on time and because customers get dissatisfied when the bundles are packaged incorrectly. Also, if loaders drive the forklifts recklessly, they damage the product and even the forklifts, which hurts profitability. Loaders affect several of the company's Performance Drivers. But, according to the company's story about winning, the loader work is not what differentiates the shipping company from its competitors. The loaders are less important than the truck drivers, strategically. The loader job is an *operator* job in the company. *Operators* are not part of your strategy for differentiating your organization, even though they are essential players in the basic operations of how your organization creates market value. Do loaders need to be strange in the same way as the truck drivers? No, the company does not need relationship building or information gathering from loaders; the loader job demands an obsession about order accuracy, safety, and punctuality.

The shipping company also employs accountants who keep the books and manage the taxes in the office. Bills need to be paid, checks received, taxes filed, and profits accurately reported, but in this company, the accounting jobs are *outsourcer* jobs. *Outsourcer* work does not help the organization create any new value for its target customers. This work is necessary to run the organization but it is not currently part of the basic operations of how the company pleases customers or beats down competitors. The results of the accounting positions do not affect the Performance Drivers listed above. The accounting workforce certainly does not need to be strange in the same way the truck drivers do. To the contrary, the shipping company wants these billing and tax preparation processes to be as normal and efficient as possible, and that is why some of these activities could be potentially outsourced. Outsourcing would allow the leaders in the shipping company to take all the energy invested into the accounting workforce (e.g., interviewing and hiring people, training and socializing employees, dealing with benefits, vacation, scheduling, and unionization threats) and reinvest it into the core workforce that differentiates the company from its competitors and creates the value for customers.

The heretical take-away here is that leaders should prioritize jobs and invest the most time, energy, and money into the positions where a strange workforce has the most leverage to make their strategies go. Even though it is not in vogue to say that some jobs are more important to the company than others, this is exactly what these questions are asking you to do. For each job in your organization, you need to understand how much it drags down strategy execution when someone messes up or acts all normal.

Question Set 2: Outsource It?

- *Why can't we just outsource this job?*

- *What Performance Drivers does this job affect?*

The point here is not to actually try and outsource all of your jobs. In fact, my guess is that you have already outsourced the positions that do not add value to your customers or your operations. The point of these questions is to get you thinking about what you expect the people in each job to deliver that isn't generic.

One of the most valuable outcomes of this discussion is that it complements your formal "job descriptions" with the real reasons different jobs exist in your company. I have found that most of the stuff written in the majority of job descriptions was written prior to the American Cival War and is generic to the point of uselessness. The leaders of the shipping company will say "we could never outsource the truck driver job—our truck drivers develop our relationships with the plant managers!" But the existing job description of "truck driver" focuses on timely deliveries and no accidents. This is what hiring decisions are based on. This is what pay is based on. Here is a situation where leaders expect unique, valuable, rare behaviors from these jobs, even though they treat the jobs and the people in the jobs just like their competitors do. Of course timely deliveries and no accidents are necessary for the truck driver job. But there is nothing strange here—these deliverables are what any truck driver in any company must do. These deliverables are necessary but not sufficient. What strange deliverables do you expect from each job in your company to make sure your unique strategy gets executed and customers notice something special about you? Try to develop strategy-based expectations for each job.

If you find a job in your organization that you have a hard time connecting to any of your Performance Drivers, there is a good chance that you should either revamp or outsource that job—even if you have always kept that job within your organization, and even if it feels uncomfortable to hire a company to do that work

> **If you find a job in your organization that you have a hard time connecting to any of your Performance Drivers, there is a good chance that you should either revamp or outsource that job.**

for you. If you can't link a job to your unique strategy for differentiating from your competitors or your basic operations, then the expectations for the job are probably generic. It is a job that is not helping your organization be remarkable to customers. It is funneling your leadership energy into being normal rather than being strange and great.

Two Things About Outsourcer Jobs

Thing 1: A job is not automatically an outsourcer just because it is not part of a profit and loss organization. If "marketing manager" means putting an ad on the newspaper, Web, and the radio, then yes, it may be an outsourcer job. If "marketing manager" means working with R&D and the sales team to create a compelling set of images that catch customers' attention, then it can be an operator or an executor position. Likewise, if "recruitment manager" means screening resumes based on GPA and creating interview schedules for managers, then yes, it is an outsourcer job. If "recruitment manager" means establishing a strange employer image among targeted job seekers so that applicants only apply when they fit the company's core values, then it can be an operator job because it helps the organization build a strange workforce that beats the competition.[2]

Thing 2: Even if a job is currently deemed an outsourcer in your organization, it does not mean it has to be or should be. You can redirect jobs and the people in those jobs to focus on new deliverables that do directly contribute to your Performance Drivers. Think hard about whether there are ways to use jobs differently to add more strategic value to your organization. Ask yourself of each outsourcer job: "What deliverables do we expect out of this job now, and what would it be possible to expect from this job that will affect our Performance Drivers? How could the people in this job do more or reprioritize their work to make our Performance Drivers move?"

[2] Cable, D. M., Aiman-Smith, L., Mulvey, P. W., & Edwards, J. R. (2000). The sources and accuracy of job applicants' beliefs about organizational culture. *Academy of Management Journal, 43*(6), 1076–1085;

Question Set 3: Specifically Strange

- *What does strange look like for this job based on our strategy?*

- *What are the characteristics of people in this job that differentiate our organization from a customer perspective?*

The point here is to keep your eye on building strange into your workforce, so that you are focused on the ways that people holding this job in your organization need to be distinct from the people your competitors put in this job. Stay away from generic job descriptions and be searching for any, differentiating characteristics that are necessary to affect your Performance Drivers. What do people in this job do to make your organization remarkable? What should your employees do in this job that your competitors would not *want* their employees to do? What would be created by this job to make your customers notice and tell some of their friends about the interaction?

The process you need to go through to answer this set of questions is basically the same as trying to figure out your workforce-wide deliverables, which we covered in the last chapter (see pp. 155-172). The difference, of course, is that now instead of discussing your whole workforce, you need to discuss each particular job. Being able to define and measure strange is most important for executor jobs and least important for outsourcer jobs.

> **Being able to define and measure strange is most important for executor jobs and least important for outsourcer jobs.**

Question Set 4: Measurement and Metrics

- *How do I measure the Workforce Deliverables for this job, rather than just talking about them?*

- *How can I distinguish the best employee I have from the worst in terms of what they accomplish, how they act, and what they know?*

Being able to articulate the ways your workforce needs to be strange is necessary but not sufficient to execute your strategy. When the going gets tough, and your time gets stretched thin, I believe you need the discipline of measurement to keep you focused on getting what you need from your work-force to make your strategy go. There are three ways you can think about what each part of your workforce must deliver to move your Performance Drivers:

- Accomplishments

- Actions

- Knowledge

What Employees Accomplish

Based on your unique way of winning, what is the job intended to accomplish or create in the world? What are the outcomes or results of the job when it is performed according to the strategy? What visable, measurable, objective changes occur when this job is performed correctly?

For example, the call center operators of a credit card company resolve problems and answer questions when customers call. Their goal is to delight customers during this "moment of truth" by efficiently responding to the customers' needs. How does the company know this result is created? Each call is taped, and every shift each operator has calls randomly evaluated based on how pleased the customer seemed with the call. These evaluations are human judgments (an entire evaluation organization was created to score and manage this data), and the scores offer a way to distinguish operators who delight customers and solve problems from operators who do not or cannot. This data is what puts reality into the words and concepts that are the call center's strategy.

A wealth management organization's strategic goal was to increase profits by serving higher-wealth clients. A key accomplishment for the consultants was dropping lower-wealth clients and landing "big game" high-wealth clients, thus increasing the profitability of their client portfolios. It is difficult to build a workforce of consultants who are each willing and able to ease themselves out of low-value client relationships (especially long-term, comfortable relationships that competitors would think they were crazy to disrupt) and reinvest their time pursuing higher-wealth clients. Actually measuring these job deliverables makes it more likely it will happen, and helps you understand who is and who is not helping execute your strategy.

Accomplishment-oriented, results-based Workforce Deliverables some-times seem like the best metrics because

- They are objective and factual.

- They often are easier to measure and track than actions or knowledge.

- They can be directly linked to the organization's Performance Driver metrics.

So why not always just focus on what people accomplish and be done with it? Why spend time dealing with behaviors and knowledge if you can just measure results? Three reasons. First, it is difficult to use accomplishment data to help individuals who do not produce the desired accomplishments because you do not have information on what they need to change in order to help you win. Second, the results of a job often depend on a set of behaviors done across a set of jobs, and attributing all of the credit to one job may be invalid and misleading. Finally, you want information on how the people *got* the results because people often game metrics and get short-term results in a way that creates long-term value destruction. For these three reasons, it is also important to gather data on how employees act and what employees know.

How Employees Act

By "act" I am talking about how employees move their arms and legs and say certain things in ways that customers notice and like. Strange workforce behaviors are at the heart of strategy execution because results are not accom-plished magically. If customers are going to notice something different about your organization that they find remarkable enough to come back with their money and friends, it usually has something to do with a group of employees acting in a valuable way that the competitors aren't willing or able to act.

Translating your competitiveness ideas into the behaviors of a workforce that change the real world is a magical thing. It's a true act of leadership. As a leader, you will rise or fall based on your ability to convert your strategy into strange behavioral expectations that affect the way customers think about your organization. Together, the different behaviors across the differ-ent jobs should affect your Performance Drivers.

> **As a leader, you will rise or fall based on your ability to convert your strategy into strange behavioral expectations that affect the way customers think about your organization.**

Do you see why this is exciting? Do you see why this all has been worth your time and energy? We are finally inside the mysterious black box with a flashlight! If your workforce acts normally in their jobs, then your workforce will not be remarkable to customers. If you want to inject something special into your products and services, then you need to do these things:

- Examine each job and determine the unique employee actions and behaviors that make or break the customer experience according to your strategy.

- Figure out ways to measure the strategic behaviors.

- Build an organization around gathering and managing data about the strategic behaviors.

Getting Better

Novant Health is a not-for-profit, integrated healthcare system in western North Carolina that serves more than 3.4 million people in 32 counties. Novant's imperative is to give world-class treatment to patients in 1929 licensed beds, not only from a medical care perspective but also from a customer experience perspective. In fact, research shows that many patients believe that all health care providers give the same level of care. Level of care is table stakes and does not help Novant differentiate or get a competitive advantage. Using focus groups, leaders studied the patient experience and highlighted critical places where competitors fail and where they are willing and able to succeed. You probably already know a lot of these hospital failure points from personal experience: Check-in is hostile, hard to understand, and time-consuming (they don't call you a *patient* for nothing!); staff is impersonal and gruff, from telephone receptionists to nurses; and the options available in the hospital rooms are difficult to understand (TV, nurse call, food timing, and food choice).

Novant leaders worked with employee focus groups on these hang-ups and tried to rethink the behaviors that people can exhibit in their jobs to improve the patient experience. First, they identified classes of behaviors that could help differentiate the hospital from its competitors. The resulting list sounds good but is abstract...courtesy, commitment, communication, etc. Probably all the other hospitals that fail in the service area talk about those concepts, too. What differentiates Novant is that they script the physical behaviors that employees should perform to make a difference with customers. For example, for any telephone interactions, the concepts were translated to include:

- Answer the phone within three rings.

- Smile as you talk because that energy "shows through" to the customer.

- Ask for permission and wait for an answer before putting someone on hold.

- Provide updates every 45 seconds for on-hold callers.

Likewise, Novant translated their concepts into personal interactions with customers that included:

- Welcome people with a smile when you greet them because when people feel welcomed, they are more likely to use our services again. A smile makes both you and the customer feel better.

- Learn people's names and address people by name; do not think of or refer to people as a diagnosis, a procedure, or a room number.

- Escort people, including patient's families and visitors, to their destinations when help is needed. This reduces frustration and makes them feel important.

- If you don't know the answer to a question, find someone who does. It is OK to say, "I don't know and I will find out," but not OK to say, "It's not my job."

As a customer, these are types of specific behaviors make a difference in your impression of the organization. By scripting, practicing, and modeling these behaviors with employees across jobs and making these behaviors an expectation about specific behaviors rather than elusive concepts like "courtesy," Novant is translating strategy into a reality that customers notice and care about. When leaders translate MBA-speak concepts about differentiating into physical, measurable behaviors that employees can understand, role play, and act out in the workplace, strategy gets turned into success.

What Employees Know

The goal here is to think about, for each job, any unique stuff employees need to have in their heads to make your organization seem like a different type of experience from a customer perspective. What can you measure in order to understand whether the knowledge is where it needs to be in your workforce?

Deposit This

A bank is trying to compete through "old-school banking" and branch loyalty. The strategy revolves around strange "bank tellers"—more specifically, bank tellers who become full-service relationship managers. The idea is that when you first go into a bank branch as a customer, you meet with a customer service associate to open an account and get set up. You get $5 deposited in your account if you fill out a brief survey about how the transaction was handled. The next time you go in to make a deposit, the associate tries to make eye contact and smiles and waves. If he is available and is not helping another customer, he flags you over and handles your banking transaction for you. When you want to buy a house, you call the branch and are funneled into an appointment with the same person, and he walks you through the loan application and the decisions about different loan products. The bank offers a car-buying service that guarantees the lowest prices, and when you call to buy a car you are funneled into a conversation with the same person, and he again walks you through the process, including the car loan itself if you need it. When you want to open a 529 for your child, you go and meet with the same person. Across time and transactions, you develop a solid, comfortable relationship with this person, and you continue to not only use that bank, but that particular bank branch.

This strategy depends, of course, on the knowledge level of the bank tellers-turned-full-service representatives (and an extremely low rate of turnover in this job). The day you set up an appointment to buy a car and your contact tells you, "Sorry, I don't know how to do that. You need to talk to Patty Black," is the day the strategy dies. The day that your contact walks you through the house loan process and you feel like he is faking is the day the strategy dies. No knowledge, no strategy execution.

As the bank leader who is spearheading this strategic initiative, how might you go about measuring which tellers have the knowledge to be deemed full-service representatives? What are some of your options? You could give each teller a test that asked the questions they would need to know to conduct all the transactions. This would give each associate a numeric score, and these scores might be considered reflections of your "strategic readiness" from a knowledge perspective. Good idea, perhaps more valid and tailored than how most organizations measure workforce knowledge, but perhaps also a lot of error. For example, you might find that lots of the tellers who do fine on the tests do not really convey confidence when they are face to face with clients, which is when it matters.

Another option would be for each branch manager to role play the full series of possible transactions with each associate, including some probing, detailed questions in each area ("Should I go with the fixed rate or ARM mortgage on a second home?"). The branch manager could score the answers, as well as the overall confidence the associate conveyed, on a standardized questionnaire. This may be better than the first approach, but since it is the branch manager, there might be self-fulfilling prophecies that influence the data (a favorite teller gets the benefit of the doubt regardless of knowledge), and there also are issues with the comparability of the scores across branches (some managers are harsh, some lenient; some blow it off, some take it seriously).

Perhaps an even better way to gauge your strategic readiness would be to form a team that knew each of the transactions very well, was trained in a structured role play that would put a bank associate through the paces and would be able to score in a consistent manner. This team could go to each bank branch and meet with each associate and produce valid, meaningful evaluation data that was comparable across branches. In addition to the ability to conduct the transactions, this team also could rate each associate's *willingness* to make this strategic change and take on the expanded role. As a leader, you could aggregate the scores and use this data to understand whether each branch were willing and able to execute your strategy.

No, this data does not guarantee your strategy would be a success—it could still be a dumb strategy if what customers really want is Internet banking. But given this *is* your strategy and you believe it is a risk worth taking, the data would give you the power to do more than hope that your workforce has the necessary knowledge to execute your strategy.

Like much of this book, this really is "Master of the Obvious" material we are covering here, right? "Tell employees the way they need to act and make sure they know what they need to know." Sometimes I wish this stuff was more complex. How can it be possible for these obvious ideas to give you a competitive advantage? It's because of how hard it is to actually *do*, and how rarely it occurs. Let's talk about why.

Fine Lines and Grounded Strategy

It takes great acts of leadership to make strategy happen in a way customers notice because it is very hard to convert big-think strategy into meaningful behaviors for employees. To execute your strategy, employees need to know how they should start behaving differently, what they should keep doing the same, and what they should stop doing altogether. A major reason this conversion from strategy to behaviors is so hard is that there are very fine lines between what behaviors you do and don't mean by your strategy.

Here is the amazing part: You cannot usually figure out these fine lines in a strategy meeting. To learn about the fine lines, you first need to get out of the corporate conference room and go work with actual employees and customers on what the strategy-appropriate behaviors look like. You need to begin observing, obsessing about, and measuring the strategic behaviors in actual job contexts. You need to hold focus groups with employees and customers, role play interactions, and watch for unintended behaviors to develop.

I call this your grounded strategy: A grounded strategy is one in which you work with employees and customers and get fine-grained in your analysis of strategy-appropriate and strategy-inappropriate behaviors, and you figure out the best way to measure the behaviors.

Then after you figure out these fine lines, you will need to draw and re-draw them for your employees. By definition, employees are not used to acting in strange ways, and you need to show them very deliberately how not to act normal. Grounding your strategy will absorb an obscene amount of time and energy, and I'm here to convince you it is *exactly* where you want to be investing your time and energy. Otherwise, a strategy is just wishful thinking in a corporate office, not a remarkable experience that is profoundly valuable to customers.

> **A grounded strategy is one in which you work with employees and customers and get fine-grained in your analysis of strategy-appropriate and strategy-inappropriate behaviors, and you figure out the best way to measure the behaviors.**

Fine Lines and Grounded Strategy at Home Depot

In Chapter 1, "Be Strange. Be Very Strange," I described Home Depot's approach to developing customer loyalty by hiring aisle associates who knew home improvement products and processes so that they could help customers solve home improvement problems. Based on this strategy, do you think aisle associates should know how to plumb if they are working in the plumbing aisle? Yes. OK, that was an easy one to start with, no fine lines there. Next question: Should a plumbing associate help customers solve their plumbing problems and try to build rapport? There's a fine line here that may not be obvious in a corporate strategy meeting, outside of an actual store. It turns out that the aisle associate should be *available* to help customers (approach the customer and ask, "Can I help with anything?"), should be *knowledge-able* about plumbing (be able to identify and fix leaks in a plumbing model), and should *offer* to help solve customer problems. But while building rapport is great, leeching behavior is bad. Aisle associates should not force their opinions on customers who clearly are not interested. Aisle associates should not bother customers with stories about the last time they plumbed their own home when customers are trying to escape. I've been a victim to these behaviors and they destroy value (and my time).

Does Home Depot really need to *measure* the extent to which aisle associates act according to the fine lines of the strategy? It depends on how important it is for this job to differentiate Home Depot for customers. If this is what winning depends on, then it sure seems important to gather data on these behaviors. How could leaders get this data? One option is hiring mystery shoppers who move through the store and evaluate the associates' behaviors (including the ability to find employees when they are needed and see how they respond to fine line situations). Another option would be to have aisle associates wear wireless transmitters so that all conversations with customers are recorded and a random number of interactions each day are evaluated, with each associate receiving a score after each shift. Would these data options be expensive and time consuming? Yes, but this is not the right question—the real question is whether Home Depot really needs these strange behaviors from the aisle associates or not.

Summary

Do you want to understand your ability to execute your strategy? Then figure out what strange accomplishments, behaviors, and knowledge you really need from each of your jobs and figure out a way to measure whether you are getting them from your workforce. To convert a strategy into a strange workforce that pleases and surprises customers, leaders need their strategies to be grounded, and they need to clearly draw the fine lines between right and wrong behaviors for employees again and again until everyone understands the differences. This type of scripting and practicing fine lines should start with the individuals in each executor job and work toward each operator job. The goal is for each employee to appreciate the special sauce that makes the company win, the strange ways they must act to help the company win, and the fine lines between behaviors that would enact versus destroy the strategy.

In the next chapter, we focus on how to go about getting your strange workforce. What levers are you going to pull to develop the workforce with the special sauce? It isn't going to happen coincidentally. You know that already. So let's do something about it.

7

Strange Workforce Architecture: What Systems Will Produce the Deliverables I Need From My Workforce?

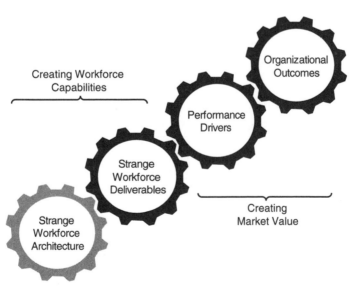

Figure 7.1   Workforce Architecture and your Strange Workforce Value Chain

If you want to build a great organization, you need to build a strange work-force using distinctive processes that employees notice early and often so that they obsess about the things that customers care about the most. Your processes should signal loud and clear to your job applicants and employees that "…around here we obsess about this particular thing, and you shouldn't be here unless that appeals to you." Here are three pieces of logic that can make a strange workforce architect out of you:

1. **Your strategy just sits on a shelf without your work-force making it happen in the real world of your customers.** If you want customers to like your products and services better than your competitors', then your work-force should deliver something unique, valuable, and hard to imitate. Your workforce doesn't need to be perfect in every way, but they do need to bring some special sauce to your customers.

2. **Your workforce will not get the special sauce by magic or coincidence—a strange workforce has to be created deliberately to serve strategic needs.** This means that if you want special sauce from your workforce, you need to become an architect of the systems that *create* your work-force. You need to be in the business of crafting systems to manage the people who achieve your Performance Drivers. You will know your systems are right when they lead to a workforce that obsesses about the things your customers care about, leaving the competition stunned and wishing they could.

3. **Your workforce won't be strange if you create it using normal approach.** If your workforce systems are just like everyone else's, it would be silly to expect any unique value or special sauce from your workforce. Serviceable, standard, normal systems that do not make employees say, "Wow!" result in a serviceable, standard, normal work-force that does not make *customers* say, "Wow!" Your methods for dealing with your workforce should be defi-nitely out of the ordinary and unexpected; unusual or strik-ing; slightly odd or even a bit weird. Your people systems need to be as strange as the workforce you hope to create.

Figure 7.2   What's competitive about being like everyone else?

What's Up with the Word "Architecture?"

Architecture deals with principles of design and construction. Functional architecture must incorporate some very basic elements (floor, walls, roof, door), and an architect must make many decisions about the design of each element. No single design decision is paramount—the whole system of design decisions must work together to succeed. A good architect cannot just consider the pitch of the roof, the layout of the floor, or whether the walls are stone or wood. What matters is how each of these elements comes together to achieve both a functional space and a social image that matches the architect's goal.

To build and manage a workforce so that you get your special sauce to beat the competition, you need to design and construct a system. This is your Workforce Architecture. What are the most basic functional elements of a Workforce Architecture?

- Get the right people to join the organization.

- Get people to know what is expected from them.

- Get people willing to work toward what is expected from them.

- Get people able to produce what is expected from them.

- Get the right people to stay and the wrong people to leave.

When an architect just copies everybody else's designs, the resulting structure does not get much attention. Nobody would call the result great, and nobody would be very inspired by it. What is called great is something unique that adds the elements together in a new way that makes the observer say, "Wow!" My goal in the next three chapters is to make your organization do something strange and effective across these five bullets so that your design elements come together in a noticeable way to achieve your Workforce Deliverables. Construct your Workforce Architecture well, and all of your people management systems add up to one strange edifice that gets noticed early and often. No one design decision is paramount—the architecture as a whole must result in a workforce that obsesses on the right things.

> **Construct your Workforce Architecture well, and all of your people management systems add up to one strange edifice that gets noticed early and often.**

Workforce Architecture Does Not Always Mean "Formal HR Processes"

You might think through the traditional HR functions (recruiting, pay, training, and the rest) and make sure you are doing something noticeable in each of them. But many effective design decisions I have seen are not what most people consider to be "formal" or "traditional" HR processes.

For example, one leader created weekly meetings where team members brief the other teams and the supervisors about last week's performance results and upcoming issues that could affect performance. This is not part of the company's "HR function," and it is not part of the formal "performance appraisal process," but it is a very salient workforce management system that has a significant effect on showing new employees what is expected, getting people motivated to achieve, and making it uncomfortable for poorly performing employees. This process demands a lot from the teams every week and builds some obsession around performance metrics.

Another example: A principal in a high school personally sits in one teacher's class each day, take notes, and then offers feedback on what was working and what was not working. When she finds a motivated teacher who is having trouble presenting content (often the case for new teachers), the principal makes time in the schedules so the teacher can go observe successful teachers of this content at other schools in the district. These two design features of the Workforce Architecture are not formal, traditional HR processes, but they are *very* unique and noticeable to teachers at the school, and they have a dramatic effect on four of the five architecture elements listed earlier.

Here's another case in point: Novant Health executives take special pains to be very visible and very vocal in obsessing about customer satisfaction in the hospitals. For example, they do "senior-level rounding," meaning that all senior-level executives get out into the care-giving facilities for one day every two weeks. During rounding, a senior executive walks up to a nurse and says, "Tell me about your customer satisfaction scores. I'm interested in learning how you are doing this month." After hearing the scores, the leader says, "Talk to me a little about the drivers of customer satisfaction in your area. What do you do to make people happy with Novant?" After learning what the nurse says about drivers, the leader asks, "Where are those results posted? I'd be interested in seeing your results last month compared to the last six months—can you show me those?" All senior-level executives make their rounds to different stations and different facilities every two weeks, the rotation shifts are formally scheduled and assigned, and the questions that executives ask are scripted to reflect the passion of the organization and what leadership is trying to influence and work on at that time. The leaders translate each of these rounding interactions into scores and notes, which are discussed in leadership meetings. When executives find a low score and lack of understanding on any employee's part about his role in making Novant great, they schedule a discussion *the next day* with that employee's direct manager to explain how the employee was unclear about his objectives or results

("Let's talk about what you're doing with your employees to ensure that they understand how they help us win…"). The CEO and the COO of a hospital also personally come to the training and orientation session of *every* new employee hired to share their excitement about how Novant is different and discuss the particular role that the new employee will play in helping Novant win. After the executives leave, newcomers often say things like, "That has never happened to me before. Upper-level administration has never talked to me at any hospital where I've worked."

Notice that these examples are not formal "HR processes," but they have a striking effect on workforce obsession and deliverables. The point here is that you need to be inventive and not constrained by traditional HR silos (pay, hiring, and the rest). You need to think hard about your Workforce Deliverables and take some irregular, even risky actions to build and focus your workforce on differentiating and winning. If achieving your Workforce Deliverables were your whole business, I'll bet you would get innovative and dedicated to acting in ways that really made sense to you, even if the rest of the world were not acting that way. You would take some risks in order to win. Guess what? Getting your workforce to deliver is your whole business. Now how are you going to go about making it happen?

> **Getting your workforce to deliver is your whole business.**

Welding a World-Class Workforce

The Lincoln Electric Company designs and manufactures arc-welding products, robotic welding systems, and plasma and oxyfuel cutting equipment in Cleveland, Ohio. Lincoln has been called "the last real welding company" and has been dedicated to welding for 107 years. Like many companies, Lincoln's strategy is to drive profits and sales by focusing their workforce on product innovation, continuous quality and productivity improvement, and industry-leading customer service and support. Lincoln needs an agile workforce obsessed with quality and productivity who thrive in a fast-paced manufacturing environment.[1]

---

[1] http://www.lincolnelectric.com/corporate/career/; Maciariello, J. A. 2000. *Lasting Value: Lessons from a Century of Agility at Lincoln Electric.* New York: John Wiley.

It is not strange for a manufacturing firm to *want* these Performance Drivers and this type of workforce, just like lots of people would like to stop smoking or lose ten pounds. What is strange is what Lincoln is willing to *do* in order to get it. Unlike most other companies, Lincoln has achieved these Performance Drivers decade after decade by creating a very strange relationship with its employees. In other words, to get a workforce that is extraordinary, Lincoln was willing to create a Workforce Architecture that was out of the ordinary, unusual, and striking. Here are three cornerstones of Lincoln Electric's Strange Workforce Architecture:

- **Lincoln guarantees lifetime employment to workers**. How's that for strange? To achieve continuous quality and productivity improvement, Lincoln needs employees' input about how to innovate products and work processes. But in most companies, when employees think up ways to increase productivity, it means less work is available and some employees will be unnecessary—not so at Lincoln, where the lifetime guarantee of employment was instituted in 1959 so employees would not have to worry about innovating themselves out of a job. Lincoln has not, in fact, had a layoff since that time. After a three-year mutual approval period, Lincoln gives a new employee their lifetime employment guarantee. But it's a two-way street because Lincoln extracts an extraordinary level of workforce flexibility in return for being strange enough to make an employment guarantee. Lincoln employees accept that they will have to work more (as many as 55 hours a week) when there is more work, and they will have to work less (as few as 30 hours per week) when work is scarce. The Lincoln workweek varied across this entire range over a two-year period in the early 1980s and has made several shorter trips below 40 hours since then. Lincoln employees also accept that they may be reassigned to different jobs, depending on where the work is. Manufacturing employees may become salespeople. Managers may become manufacturing employees. For example, since he joined Lincoln after high school, foreman Bob Knapik has held 20 different jobs.[2] People are paid for the job they're doing, not the job they used to do. The pay might be

[2] Eisenberg, D., Sieger, M., & Greenwald, J. 2001. "Where People Are Never Let Go."
Time: Vol. 157 (24), p. 40-44.

more, it might be less. When Lincoln divested and sold a motor division in 1999, part of the contract in selling the business was that the buyer had to give back those employees over a two-year period. Lincoln brought every single one of those employees back into productive jobs, allowing Lincoln to keep its promises to the workforce while retaining loyal, valuable, and highly skilled employees.[3] Oh, by the way, the company that bought the motor business eventually left town, meaning that those workers would have been laid off. "I never have to wake up in the morning and wonder if I've got a job," says Bob Knapik.

- **Lincoln pays wages for quality product, not for time**. Lincoln pays factory jobs on a piecework basis, which means that an employee's pay is literally determined by the amount of quality output he or she produces. If you are a hard-working manufacturing employee and you put in an entire day boring the wrong size holes, the parts go to scrap and you go home without money for that day's work. If you don't come to work, then you aren't producing and you get no pay. So if you want to stay home on the 4th of July, or Christmas, that is fine but you receive no pay for those days. You get sick, fine, but don't expect to receive any pay if you stay home. Strange enough for you? Unlike other companies, Lincoln has huge variation in production-worker pay: from about $32,000 per year to over $100,000 for the highest producers.[4] If older workers slow down, their salaries do too. Do you think that this system attracts a workforce that is obsessed with quality and productivity who thrive in a fast-paced manufacturing environment? Do you think many unproductive employees stick around for long? Let's just say that Lincoln employees are the highest-paid manufacturing employees in the world, and you can do the math about their productivity levels. "How much money you make is in your own hands," says Thomas

---

[3] "How 'No Layoffs' Can Work." Business Week Online, 11/6/2001. This article first appeared at http://www.Business Week Online. An online version remains in the Business Week Online archives.

[4] "A Model Incentive Plan Gets Caught in a Vise." *Business Week*, January 22, 1996: Number 3459; p. 89.

Gadomski, a painting-crew leader.[5] As one production
employee said, "If you're good, you can make it here. If not,
I suggest not coming."[6]

- **Lincoln reinvests an uncommonly large percentage of company profits—for example $27,470,500[7]—into an annual bonus.** Each year, for over 73 consecutive years, Lincoln distributes a profit-sharing bonus to employees right before the Christmas holidays. Most companies might give a few hundred dollars as a bonus, some give a turkey or a ham, and some give none at all. In 2000, the average bonus at Lincoln was $17,579, about 45% of an employee's salary.[8] Combine the bonus with the unlimited ability to earn piece-rate dollars, and that's how top factory workers take home more than $100,000 a year. Each employee is rated twice a year on quality, output, dependability, cooperation, and ideas.[9] The ratings determine how much of the total corporate bonus pool each worker will get on top of his or her regular pay. Lincoln takes its bonus commitment to the employees very, very seriously. In fact, Lincoln actually borrowed more than $100 million in 1992 and 1993 to pay bonuses in the United States, even though the company lost a total of $84 million in those years due to a foreign-acquisition spree. Since U.S. operations had achieved one of its most profitable years ever, CEO Donald F. Hastings said, "I had to go to the board and say, 'We can't break our trust with this group because of management mistakes and recession elsewhere.'"[10]

---

5   "A Model Incentive Plan Gets Caught in a Vise." *Business Week*, January 22, 1996: Number 3459; p. 89.

6   *60 Minutes*. "Guaranteed Employment at Lincoln Electric: Ahead or Behind the Times?" (CBS television broadcast, Nov. 8, 1992).

7   12/12/03 CLEVELAND, Dec. 12 /PRNewswire-FirstCall/. http://phx.corporate-ir.net/phoenix.zhtml?c=100845&p=irol-newsArticle_Print&ID=541313&highlight=.

8   "Where People Are Never Let Go," p. 40.

9   Maciariello, J. A. 2000. *Lasting Value: Lessons from a Century of Agility at Lincoln Electric*. John Wiley & Sons, Inc. New York.

10   "A Model Incentive Plan Gets Caught in a Vise" p. 89.

Look at how these three strange architectural elements balance each other and work as a system. Lifetime employment doesn't work unless you have pay-at-risk and obsession with productivity and quality. Huge bonuses based on profitability don't work if employees are not implementing innovation and efficiency ideas that drive profits. Individual piece-rate incentives create competitive, lone-wolf behaviors if they are not balanced by the huge bonus based on company-level profitability, which is distributed to employees based on their contributions to their teams. The design elements of this system are mutually reinforcing—it creates a synergy that boosts overall performance.[11] This overall system gets and keeps the workforce's attention creating almost cult-like employee dedication (turnover is less than 4% among those with at least 180 days on the job). "There isn't any other place to work like Lincoln Electric," says Kathleen Hoenigman, an 18-year veteran. "They take care of you."[12]

Strange Architecture → Strange Workforce → Extraordinary Results

Lincoln's strange architecture and workforce have served the company well over the years. Despite having some of the highest-paid factory workers in the world, Lincoln Electric dominates the price-sensitive welding market, having pushed industrial powerhouses like General Electric out of the business. As of the writing of this book in 2006, their stock is up about 190% since January 2001, and since January 1995, it is up about 520%.

Lincoln's strange Workforce Architecture also has earned the company considerable public recognition. Lincoln has been favorably featured in most major media outlets, including *60 Minutes, Business Week, CNBC, PBS, Time, USA Today, The Financial Times*, and the *Harvard Business School Press*. In the past, Lincoln has given hundreds of tours to other company leaders.[13]

[11] Milgrom, P., & Roberts, J. "Complementarities and Fit Strategy, Structure, and Organizational Change in Manufacturing." *Journal of Accounting and Economics*, 1995: 19: 179-208.

[12] "A Model Incentive Plan Gets Caught in a Vise," p. 89.

[13] Byrne, J. A. 1995. "Management Meccas." *Business Week*, September 18, 122-132.

If it all works so darn well, why don't more companies do it like Lincoln
Electric? Because it takes an abnormal level of dedication and obsession to be
this strange. Most companies and leaders simply don't feel it is possible to be
that different from the normal. Doing anything as strange as offering lifetime
employment or giving most of the annual profits back to the employees as a
bonus would simply be ruled out as too crazy. It also means creating an entire
workforce system, not just picking off a thing or two that you like about
Lincoln's system. Sure, many executives like the self-funding nature of piece-
rate incentives, but you just don't get Lincoln's level of success with piece-rate
if you fail to balance it with lifetime security, the bonus scheme, and the hiring and socialization system. And get this—even if you do appreciate the
value and importance of how the various pieces of this system complement
each other, it's not going to be easy to just copy it. "It is easy to announce that
the firm will pay piece rates. It is much harder to develop credibility for a no-
layoff policy or the worker trust that Lincoln enjoys and has earned over the
last 60 years."[14] The upshot is that the Lincoln Electric architecture is valuable because it produces the workforce that they need to beat down competitors. It is rare—do you know many companies treating their workforce like
Lincoln Electric? It is hard to imitate—do you think you could imitate this
architecture? Perhaps you can see why a strange Workforce Architecture can
give a company a sustained competitive advantage.

I think you get this already, but I need to say it: The point of this chapter is not to convince you to imitate Lincoln Electric's Workforce
Architecture. Even if you *could* imitate Lincoln's exact system as a whole, it
probably wouldn't work for your organization because how you beat your
own competitors into the ground probably demands different deliverables
from your workforce. The point is to get juiced up about being strange and
winning your own way. You need to get excited and passionate about creating an architecture so valuable, rare, and hard to imitate that competitors
can't take you down even after you show them how to do it.

Don't Be So Darn Attractive to Everyone

Today's alchemy lesson: Find strange people who naturally obsess on value-
producing things, mix them into a strange organization that transforms the

[14] Milgrom, P., & Roberts, J. p. 179-208.

obsession into something that customers notice and are willing to pay for. This recipe yields a competitive advantage, but it is not magic. It is strategic, structured, and successful. Be strange enough so that not everyone wants to work in your company, just the people who are obsessed about delivering the unique value that your company is built around.

> **Be strange enough so that not everyone wants to work in your company, just the people who are obsessed about delivering the unique value that your company is built around.**

Rather than just hoping really hard that employees will be innovative and institute productivity enhancements, Lincoln is actually willing to do something very unusual to make it happen. The strange cornerstones of this Workforce Architecture—guaranteed lifetime employment, timesharing and work assignment flexibility, piece-rate pay, profit sharing as a large proportion of total pay—make Lincoln quite a strange place to work. For example, there is a sign on the front door of the factory telling employees not to show up more than 30 minutes *before* their shift's starting time. Now how strange is that?

Let's face it: Not everyone would want to work at Lincoln. In fact, *most* people would not want to work at Lincoln. That's fine—not everyone has to work there. Just the tight-knit, fiercely-loyal, obsessed tribe of 3,200 people—they look at the strange Lincoln system and say, "Wow! Now that's for me." When strange people work in a strange system that feels like it was molded for them, it feels like coming home, and their loyalty to and identification with the organization skyrockets.[15] Lincoln employees know it is strange working there, and they like it that way. It helps them identify with the organization. To the best workers in the most strategic jobs that demand the most obsession, you want your organization to feel like coming home. You want it to feel both unique and built around people's personal values, like a hand in a glove.

---

[15] Cable, D. M., & Judge, T. A. "Person-Organization Fit, Job Choice Decisions, and Organizational Entry." *Organizational Behavior and Human Behavior Processes*, 1996: 67(3), pp. 294-311.

"But We Already Have People Systems in Place"…and Other Fine Whines

When I talk about creating a strange Workforce Architecture, some leaders complain that they already have existing systems in place that would be almost impossible to change. Their existing systems are complex structures, and they have workforces built with the existing systems that are legacies of and tributes to the past. It would be really uncomfortable to make changes to them because the systems have deep roots. And many people would resist changes because the existing systems are part of the culture of their institutions. "Our existing Workforce Architecture is fine," they say.

By "fine," these leaders are not implying their existing Workforce Architecture is "characterized by elegance, refinement, and accomplishment." What they really mean is *serviceable*: Employees get hired; employees get paid—nothing too distinctive, fairly typical, and pretty uninspiring. Hmmmm. Does this sound to you like the type of system that makes employees bring feverish intensity to their jobs so that customers notice some special sauce that makes them want to give you their money? Just because a system is erstwhile doesn't mean you can let it ride if it's not resulting in a workforce that makes customers notice you.

So what are you going to do? Not differentiate? Not win? Ignoring the foundation of your differentiation is not smart. I'm not saying that you need to overhaul and implement a strange new system tomorrow. The change to strange may take years, but it won't happen if you don't start.

> **The change to strange may take years, but it won't happen if you don't start.**

Why else might you be frustrated as you read this chapter? You may not be high enough in the org chart to change promotion policies. You could be in an organization with a hiring freeze, and you cannot hire any new blood to help you win. Your boss may have given you too much day-to-day work to be fooling around with HR policies. You may have a unionized workforce that does not permit incentives or benefits to be altered. You may not have a training budget. Gee, now that I think of it, you are probably just too constrained to change your Workforce Architecture.

Listen…off in the distance. Do you hear what I hear? I think I hear your competitors laughing. I hear them rejoicing that you are giving up. The competition is just thrilled that you don't feel empowered enough to manage your workforce to greatness. The competition is giddy that your people systems have been in place so long that they have calcified and are hard to change.

> **The competition is just thrilled that you don't feel empowered enough to manage your workforce to greatness.**

What do you want to do, whine or win? Producing your Workforce Deliverables is not just a "nice to have" if you want to win. If you actually plan to take down your competition rather than just edit your strategy Powerpoint presentation again, then you need to get serious about how you are going to get the workforce you need to make your organization stand out to your customers. Sure, it will be hard to change your systems. Getting a competitive advantage needs to be hard, or it wouldn't be a sustained competitive advantage. The fact that it is hard to create a distinctive system that brings together the right group of people who are strangely focused on what customers care about means that organizations succeeding in this domain will gain a competitive advantage. These organizations will rise to greatness because this is the foundation of value creation, it is hard to do, and it is hard to imitate. If you want to build a great organization, then you need to figure out a way to be distinctive, attractive, and remarkable to the people that can make your strategy go: employees and customers.

> **Whenever you get to feeling that you have no control over your people systems, keep in mind that actually this is one of the few pieces of competitive advantage that leaders can literally, directly control.**

Whenever you get to feeling that you have no control over your people systems, keep in mind that actually this is one of the few pieces of competitive advantage that leaders can literally, directly control. You can't literally force the world to give you higher sales margins. You can't literally force customers to give you a better reputation. You can't literally force your workforce to innovate products that customers want more than the competitors'. What you *can* literally do is create a strange system that locates, hires, and motivates a workforce that innovates products that customers want more than the competitors'.

Institutionalizing Entrepreneurship Through Strange Workforce Architecture

William McKnight, president of 3M from 1929 to 1949 and then chairman from 1949 to 1966, thought hard about the strange ways the organization must think about and treat its workforce in order to differentiate and reliably succeed at profitable invention. Said McKnight:

> "Mistakes will be made, but if a person is essentially right, the mistakes he or she makes are not as serious in the long run as the mistakes management will make if it is dictatorial and undertakes to tell those under its authority exactly how they must do their job. Management that is destructively critical when mistakes are made kills initiative, and it is essential that we have many people with initiative if we are to continue to grow."[16]

Sure, all kinds of companies *talk* about creating an innovative culture by giving employees the freedom to make mistakes. But 3M became an innovation powerhouse and a Fortune 500 mainstay by dedicating itself to some strange workforce practices that incorporate random chance into company policy.[17] Example: To allow engineers and scientists to follow their instincts and interests, 3M encourages "experimental doodling." 3M engineers spend up to 15% of their work time off the grid pursuing "bootlegging" activities— defined roughly as working on whatever stuff they are obsessed with. Moreover, if capable researchers are assigned to a project that "fails," people aren't penalized but instead are moved quickly onto a new project. The idea is that to innovate, 3M must accept failure as a productive stage on the road to winning. 3M also encourages an underdog innovation spirit with Genesis Grants, an internal venture capital fund available to engineers whose ideas

---

[16] Bartlett, C. A. & Mohammed, A. "3M: Profile of an Innovating Company." *Harvard Business School*, 1995: 9-395-016.

[17] Overfelt, M. 2003. "3M." *Fortune Small Business*, 13, 36-41.

have been turned down by management. The company's "11th Commandment" is, "Thou shalt not kill a new product idea," and William McKnight told his managers, "If you put fences around people, you get sheep. Give people the room they need."

Another way 3M gives the R&D workforce some room and encourages a grassroots scientific community is investing in the Technical Forum and Annual Technology Fairs. These design elements of 3M's Workforce Architecture are closer to a science fair or an academic conference than a business meeting. They allow 3Mers to geek-out and be both scientific and voyeuristic—they show off their inventions to peers across the company while learning what new-to-the-world technologies everyone else is working on. 3M further encourages idea sharing through its approach to lab performance auditing. In this system, audit teams of scientific peers from other parts of the organizations review the current work of each lab every three years and then report their findings and recommendations to lab and division management. Six of the audit members are internal to the lab being audited, while the other six are drawn from corporate technical staff and from other 3M labs familiar with the technology under review.

3M's science and research obsession also is fostered through its promotion systems. Most companies have promotion policies that stipulate moving onto the management track if you want to move up in the company. The result is the "Peter Principal," where great R&D contributors turn themselves into mediocre managers in pursuit of advancement. To combat this unfortunate turn of events early on, 3M created one of the first dual ladder career tracks that lets researchers and engineers progress in their careers while staying true to their professional interests. Being a great product innovator and researcher is rewarded both extrinsically (promotions and raises) and intrinsically (prestige and honor). In fact, the greatest 3M achievement is being inducted into the Carlton Society, an honor reserved for those who made the most exceptional scientific contributions to the company. And every year, the company sends its top 20 scientific overachievers and their spouses on a four-day holiday at 3M's corporate retreat in Park Rapids, MN.

Once upon a time, away from 3M headquarters, sat a large, old dairy building. In 1944, it was formally named the "Products Fabrication Laboratory" but was affectionately known as the "funny farm." Lots of 3M inventions over the years occurred in the very strange, decentralized, autonomous working conditions of the funny farm. It was a makeshift laboratory and idea incubator. Like The Island of Misfit Toys, this facility was a place to call home for eccentric research underdogs with imaginative personalities and habits of tinkering, often non-degree lab techs. William McKnight installed Richard Drew—famous inside 3M for inventing Scotch tape after being told it was a dog and to stop working on it—as head of the funny farm lab. Drew populated his lab with strange people like himself, renegades who were not corporate types but who delivered amazing creativity. Drew was a better scientist, mentor, or leader than he was a manager: His mantra was that it's easier to ask forgiveness than permission. Being strange paid off for the funny farm. Drew's group developed breakthroughs for more than 20 years, including Micropore surgical tape, face masks, respirators, Tartan (a rubbery surface for athletic fields), and the early Post-it Note (not commercialized until 1980). The strange processes and successes of the funny farm showed 3M corporate leaders how an atypical organization and workforce could be a percolator of breakthrough creativity. "Drew took a bunch of misfits—people who wouldn't fly in formation—and he put them together," says Art Fry, one of the inventors of the Post-it Note. "The lab created technologies that still accounted for 20% of 3M's sales in 2000."[18]

3M does not have a perfect track record. As McKnight said, mistakes will be made. But on average, these strange design cornerstones of 3M's Workforce Architecture raise the probability of scientific experimentation and create higher-than-average obsession with innovation. Many great and profitable lines of business were created from projects that 3M researchers continued to invest bootleg time in long after management killed the formal project. In fact, the legends of the company are those who actively resisted management indifference and organizational rejection of their ideas. Talk about obsessed: Philip Palmquist defied orders to stop working on reflective sheeting and worked in his lab at night and developed the technology behind "Scotchlite™." A project team worked on insulated clothing as a bootleg business despite management's attempt to stop it (it was not deemed an "appropriate business" for 3M), culminating in 3M's highly successful Thinsulate brand. That's an obsession that customers are willing to pay for.

---

[18] Overfelt, M. 2003. "3M." *Fortune Small Business*, 13, 36–41.

And you thought they were just lucky? Nah, the 3M workforce and the profitable innovation it produces are strange by design. 3M has created "a climate that stimulates ordinary people to produce extraordinary performances."[19] It's hard to "command innovation," but 3M's Workforce Architecture and leadership induce innovation by institutionalizing strange and encouraging workforce obsession. What strange workforce obsession are you institutionalizing?

> **What strange workforce obsession are you institutionalizing?**

---

[19] Bartlett, C. A. & Mohammed, A.

8

Strange Workforce Architecture: Breaking Out From the Pack

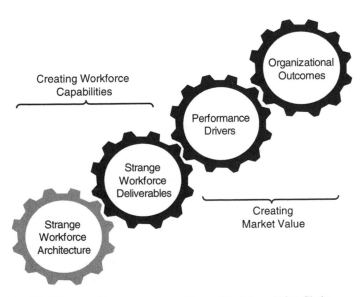

Figure 8.1 Workforce Architecture and your Strange Workforce Value Chain

The last chapter opened up the meaning of strange Workforce Architecture and tried to get you thinking some big thoughts about creating a system that your workforce (and even society) will notice. A strange Workforce Architecture is the basis of your competitive advantage if you plan on your employees creating something different from your competitors. So in some respects, it is the tap root of this book.

Remember the five core elements of a functional Workforce Architecture?

- Get the right people to join the organization.

- Get people to know what is expected from them.

- Get people willing to work toward what is expected from them.

- Get people able to produce what is expected from them.

- Get the right people to stay and the wrong people to leave.

The issue that you need to come to terms with is how, using these architectural elements, you will create the appropriate level and type of obsession in your workforce. Maybe this is an opportunity for another leadership team meeting. Maybe the output from this meeting becomes a set of deliverables for a new suborganization of your Human Resource organization. For each architectual element, you need to be able to answer the following questions:

- What do we currently do with this element to make employees say, "Wow?" What are we doing to differentiate ourselves from other employers with this element?

- If we aren't doing anything strange with this element now, how could we push it "over the top" to show the workforce that we care very, very deeply about the deliverables in this job? What are the strengths of our existing Workforce Architecture that we can build on to really get the workforce's attention?

- What do we measure to ensure that we actually have this element set up the way we want it? How can we prove that our system is strange enough to make people notice it? What evidence do we have that our system is sending the signals that we intend to the targeted people?

Create a Caricature of Your Workforce Architecture

The goal of this exercise is to envision your own distinctive Workforce Architecture that can get your organization to greatness. How do you do this? One way to jump-start this process is to think about drawing a caricature of your Workforce Architecture. A caricature is a representation in which the subject's distinctive features or peculiarities are deliberately exaggerated. You minimize features that are small on the subject and maximize features that are enlarged on the subject. So David Letterman needs huge teeth and Mick Jagger needs huge lips because you want people to immediately notice the most salient features and be able to recognize the subject. Creating a caricature forces you to decide what is most distinctive so that you can really make it stand out to viewers. As a caricaturist, you need to decide what elements contribute most to the overall image you are trying to create for the viewer, and then you need to over-emphasize those elements to make sure it stands out and gets noticed. At Lincoln Electric, it's easy to identify the truly strange components of their Workforce Architecture that get the most attention from job seekers and employees (and the media!) and that have the heaviest pull in terms of creating the strange workforce that delivers rare and hard to imitate value to customers.

> **Creating a caricature forces you to decide what is most distinctive so that you can really make it stand out to viewers.**

Try using the caricature analogy to think about the design of your Workforce Architecture. Here are some issues to consider as you move forward:

- **Decide what will really "pop."** What is strange enough about your system to make job seekers and new employees think, "Wow, this seems different!" What is strange enough to make experienced employees tell friends who want to apply for a job, "It's definitely not for everyone; we do things pretty differently than what you're used to."

- **Accentuate existing features.** Hopefully, you already have architectural elements in place that help make you stand out to current and potential employees, that get you the special sauce you need from your workforce, and that you are proud of. I'm sure you could find ways to underscore them a little more to really work the strange angle. But these existing strengths are organizational treasures to be protected and built around and supported by your other decisions.

WARNING

Just because one of your people systems has a rich heritage in your company, it does not guarantee it is a strength. For example, you may be proud of being the "pay leader" in an industry. It is in fact strange to pay more than is necessary, and you may think that this design feature is netting you the smartest and most driven job seekers. But if you do not have evidence that job seekers actually perceive your organization as a pay leader, then you may not be getting a bang for your buck. If you do not have evidence that the best applicants take jobs with you rather than your competitors due to over-payment, then your investment may be in vain because your theory of strange is not supported. It's important to know and not just hope.

- **CYA: Cover your architecture.** Try to think about and describe two or three strange, visible "cornerstone" design features that together cover all five of the architectural elements. The right people join; people know what is expected; people are *willing* to achieve; people are *able* to achieve; the right people to stay and the wrong people leave. Each cornerstone design feature doesn't need to cover each of the five elements, but as a system the whole set of elements should be covered.

- **Keep focused on Workforce Deliverables.** Remember, in your caricature, you need to keep the strange stuff focused on what it takes to win. Workforce Architecture cannot be strange just for the sake of being strange, or getting attention, or having fun. Your Workforce Architecture needs to be strange in a way that makes your workforce strange in a way that customers notice, appreciate, and pay for. This is why our

Workforce Value Chain started with winning and why you must build your strange architecture around your Workforce Deliverables that we uncovered in Chapters 5 and 6. So even if you currently have a design feature that is noticeable and is part of your culture, you may need to adapt it or dissolve it if it doesn't get you what you need from your workforce.

- **The system has to work as a system.** Once you include three or four very noticeable features in your caricature, stand back from it and make sure it "works" as a whole. Do the strange features complement, balance, and reinforce each other as one cohesive system? As a system, will it capture employees' attention and steer them directly toward your Workforce Deliverables? Like a caricature, all the features should come together as a single distinctive image that is noticeable and recognizable to the viewer. Lifetime security wouldn't work for Lincoln Electric without extraordinary levels of pay-at-risk. Making Whole Foods teams select newcomers "off the island" wouldn't work without team-based pay (see the "Strange Foods" section at the end of this chapter).

Make Your Architecture Conform to the Strange Elements

Once you commit to a few strange cornerstone features of your Workforce Architecture, then something very useful happens. Your strange elements start to make demands on *other* parts of the architecture in a way that forces you to upgrade and evolve the system as a whole to make the strange features work. To be honest, these repercussions may seem like work that you don't really want to get involved with right now. However, it's important to take the long view and remember that *this is helpful*. Here's an analogy—for those of us who have renovated old houses, we call it the "one thing leads to another" phenomenon. Originally, you just want to unstick a window. But as you're burning off the old paint, you discover that some of the wood is weak and papery from termite damage. As you pull off the wood to replace it, you discover that water has been penetrating and collecting inside the window sill, and you uncover some substantial termite damage in the support joists. And before you know it, your two-hour project has evolved into a three-day journey and nine trips to the home improvement store. Of course you are very tempted to just fill the wood with Bondo, slap some paint on it, and not dig into the core problem. This, however, would not be an intelligent move. The real goal is to renovate the house, not to get done with the window project. It's better to address the problem now than let water and termites destroy your house.

Do you see how the "one thing leads to another" phenomenon might occur as you are renovating your Workforce Architecture? For example, after a principal of a high school decides to randomly observe and give feedback to her teachers on a daily basis (a strange, attention-getting tactic), she realizes she needs to clarify her model of what good versus bad teaching performance looks like (accomplishments, behaviors, and knowledge). After the principal decides to send failing teachers around to other school districts to shadow other teachers and improve (a strange, attention-getting tactic), she realizes she needs to invest the time learning what teachers at other schools are doing things right. Once the principal identifies and partners with teachers at other schools who are doing things right, she discovers some ways to make her own school stand out to *those* teachers as a great place to work, which creates a great new recruitment source.

Plugging a few strange "cornerstones" into your Workforce Architecture helps point out what else needs to happen to make it hang together and work as a system. So what does this mean for you? It means your caricature should prioritize the two or three distinctive design decisions that you truly want to pop, and then you can—slowly, perhaps—backfill the rest of your Workforce Architecture so that it results in a cohesive system that could actually be used to manage your workforce.

> **Plugging a few strange "cornerstones" into your Workforce Architecture helps point out what else needs to happen to make it hang together and work as a system.**

You also will find that a single strange design feature will span several of the basic elements of a Workforce Architecture. For example, Lincoln Electric's piece-rate plan helps get the right people to join the organization (because people who are not confident in their high productivity would likely not select into the company in the first place[1]). Employees know what is expected from them early, due to the piece-rate plan's basis on production quality and quantity (and the fact that this system has created a strong set of behavioral norms at Lincoln). The piece-rate plan makes the types of people who sign up to work at Lincoln highly motivated to contribute the right behaviors (because they will not be paid otherwise). Finally, it is unlikely that low performers would stay at Lincoln (given that the piece-rate plan would not pay for their attendance if they were not producing), while the best workers who are making north of $100,000 without a college degree are unlikely to find better alternatives elsewhere. This is why a caricature containing just two or three strange design features can hit all five core elements of a Workforce Architecture.

The upshot: Use a few well-designed strange elements to lead you to a holistic Workforce Architecture that looks and feels strikingly different to employees and that gets you what you need from your workforce to make customers notice.

Figure 8.2   Use noticeable people systems to cook up your special sauce

---

[1]   Cable, D., & Judge, T. A. "Pay Preferences and Job Search Decisions: A Person-Organization Fit Perspective." *Personnel Psychology*, 1994: 47, pp. 317-348.

Hire the Best and the Strangest

Lots of organizations claim that they "hire the best and the brightest." But in reality, most organizations act like most other organizations. Few are willing and able to actually be strange enough to hire the people who make up a workforce that is strangely willing and able to impress customers. The problem is that if you mess up and hire someone who doesn't bring the special sauce, then you spend the rest of the relationship trying to fight the person and fix a problem you created yourself.

In Chapter 1, "Be Strange. Be Very Strange," we took a peek at the strange tribe of mechanics at General Electric's Durham Engine Facility (DEF). Now, let's look at how strange they get when it's time to hire someone for a team. First, the mechanics from the teams who have rotated into the HR role go out to external career fairs with the plant's HR support person. In their presentations to job seekers, the mechanics are very open with specific examples about what is thrilling and what is difficult about working at the DEF. For example, after one mechanic talked about the team doing their own scheduling and not having a manager to look after them, a potential applicant sitting in the recruiting session said, "That must be great, not having a boss!" To which the GE mechanic responded, "What are you talking about? It's more like having eight bosses. I have eight people watching my behavior all day every day. If I'm causing any problems, all eight of them will let me know about it." Most of the GE mechanics have worked in traditional manufacturing settings, and they give lots of detail about how it's different to work at the DEF. To the potential applicants, this presentation comes off very different than listening to a canned talk from an HR rep who had never held a mechanic job. It's strange how important these signals are to job seekers.[2]

Once 12 solid applicants with an FAA license apply for the opening, the real work begins. From 6:45am until 3:00pm, six mechanics who have received extensive training to be assessors, along with HR support, put the group of 12 candidates through the paces. They work through structured group role plays, assembly exercises, writing procedures, business case analyses, and structured panel interviews. Eight hours of evaluation! The

---

[2] Rynes, S., Bretz, R. D., & Gerhart, B. "The Importance of Recruitment in Job Choice: A Different Way of Looking." *Personnel Psychology*, 1991: 44, pp. 487-521.

eight hours is spent collecting data about how the applicants would fit into the job and the DEF culture, and each step of this process is linked to the specific flavor of strange that GE is trying to build in its workforce.

For example, in one exercise, the 12 applicants are divided into two teams of six and placed at two tables on opposite sides of the room. Each applicant has some plastic Lego building blocks in front of him. In the front of the room, there is a screen. The candidates are told, "On the other side of that screen is a model helicopter made out of Legos. Your team has five trips to send someone to study the helicopter and come back to communicate what he or she saw. Your goal is to build the helicopter, but you are not permitted to touch each other's Lego pieces. You have 30 minutes. Go." Three mechanics and an HR support person observe each team, scoring each of the applicants on clipboards. What do you think the scores are based on? Well, since the applicants know they are being evaluated, it is very common for one of them to try to "demonstrate leadership" and "take initiative" by jumping up first and going behind the screen. This unilateral action is scored as a negative behavior by the observers because that is not how a team works together at the DEF. The applicant who gets the most points is the one who says something like, "Let's try to come up with a plan, here. Who has kids and plays with these things?" At GE's DEF, being a leader is not a lone-wolf activity; it is a collaborative affair, and everyone must work as a team. Often, an applicant will go behind the screen, look at the model helicopter, come back to the team, and say, "I can't remember what I saw!" Not remembering is not nearly as important to the judges as how the applicant's team members react to the not remembering. Some applicants will roll their eyes disgustedly or mutter under their breath (they assume their job offer hangs on being able to replicate the helicopter, and now this dufus is screwing it up)—they receive negative scores for these reactions. Other applicants will say, "It's OK, think for a minute…do you remember any of the colors above the rotor?" This type of positive communication and drawing out information and is scored positively by the observers. Having the teams "compete" to build the helicopter usually creates some drive and stress to get it done first. But in the end, it actually does not matter if a team completes the helicopter or not. What matters is how the applicants behave toward one another and how those actions translate into the Workforce Deliverables that are required in DEF's self-managed teams.

Do you think that this data on applicants' communication and teamwork are more valid than, say, asking them in an interview, "Do you communicate well as part of a team in stressful conditions?" Applicants' behavioral reactions in the DEF setting are more likely to reflect their natural, innate tendencies, not what they are savvy enough to say in an interview. Later, in the hiring meeting, the evaluators compare their scores to make sure agreement was high and that someone was not missing something important. Do you think that these scores, which are based on how the applicants would fit in to the strange conditions at the DEF, are more predictive of success than an interview? Do you think that having the mechanics do the judging and the selection leads to better decisions and more commitment to the new hires than if HR ran the whole process? Do you think that most organizations make this kind of commitment to hiring the best? Nope—it's strange.

In another exercise, applicants sit at a table with an engine from one of those scaled model airplanes that people fly in big open fields. The applicants also are given a tool set and a computer. They are told to "take the engine apart, put it back together, and write up the directions for how to build it. You have one hour. Go." Each applicant's assembly directions that result from this exercise are scored for clarity, logic, and accuracy. The rebuilt airplane engines are tested for functionality. Do you think the scores resulting from this exercise might be more valid than how hiring decisions get made in most organizations—reading an applicant's resume and talking abstractly during an interview?

At GE's DEF, the eight hours of applicant assessment does *not* include the setup in the morning (another hour) and does *not* include the very heated debate about who to hire when all the applicants go home (always four more hours, sometimes six or more hours). Why does it take so long? First, to receive a job offer, an applicant has to clear a minimum bar across each and every evaluation category (minimum of a 4/7 on every category). And, hiring at the DEF is based on consensus decision-making, which means that all the judges need to agree. A single team member who saw something troubling can veto a job offer. There are many times when not one of the 12 applicants clears the absolute bar across all judges, and no offers are made. This is a tremendous commitment to making the right decision. Sound strange to you? Do you think this approach gives the DEF higher-quality individuals who create higher-quality team output?

With a full day of these types of exercises and events, the DEF's hiring process clearly sends a signal to job applicants. This hiring process turns off many "normal" mechanics, as their undesirable attitudes are exposed during the course of the day and are picked out by the judges. Some applicants even voluntarily leave before finishing the day. The Durham Engine Facility considers this self-selection a positive event. You should too. You do not want normal hiring processes that attract normal people. You do not want to be an employer of choice to everyone. Only certain types of people should be attracted to your organization—those who are themselves strange in the way that your workforce is strange.

> Only certain types of people should be attracted to your organization—those who are themselves strange in the way that your workforce is strange.

GE's Durham Engine Facility demonstrates that when you get serious about hiring a strange workforce, you win in three ways:[3]

- You differentially attract people who are hard-wired to make your strategy go.

- Your careful selection processes ensure that new hires are as strange as your organization. This is how you give the gift of organizational fit to new hires, which is a unique reward that bonds them to your organization in a way that competitors cannot imitate. It feels like coming home.

---

[3] Cable, D. M., Aiman-Smith, L., Mulvey, P. W., & Edwards, J. R. (2000). "The sources and accuracy of job applicants' beliefs about organizational culture." *Academy of Management Journal*, 43(6), 1076-1085;

Cable, D. M., & Judge, T. A. (1996). "Person-organization fit, job choice decisions, and organizational entry." *Organizational Behavior and Human Behavior Processes*, 67(3), 294-311;

Cable, D. M., & Turban, D. (2001). "Recruitment image equity: Establishing the dimensions, sources, and value of job seekers' organizational beliefs." In G. R. Ferris (Ed.), *Research in Personnel and Human Resources Management* (Vol. 20, pp. 115-163). Greenwich, CT: JAI Press; Schneider, B. (1987). "The people make the place." *Personnel Psychology*, 40, 437-453.

- People who do not fit your strategy are repelled by the strange-ness and save you the pain of their misdeeds and the trouble of firing them.

So do you think that my point is that you should copy the hiring systems of the Durham Engine Facility? No, not any more than you should copy Lincoln Electric's incentive plan. This is the myth of best practices: You will proba-bly not be able to imitate your way to greatness. Your own strange systems have to be created around the obsessions and unique abilities you need from your workforce.

My point is that you should be conducting *some* strange practices across *some* of the elements of your Workforce Architecture. I want to get you inspired that creating a strange, noticeable Workforce Architecture is very costly but worth it when it delivers the Workforce Deliverables that are your organization's competitive advantage. You want to invest so deeply in getting the right workforce that competitors are stunned. They'll want your results (Organizational Outcomes), but they won't be willing or able to do what it takes to *get* the results. You want your ignorant competitors to look at your systems and say, "That's stu-pid," and you want your smart competitors to say, "We could never do that."

> **You want your ignorant competitors to look at your systems and say, "That's stupid," and you want your smart competitors to say, "We could never do that."**

Strange Foods

"The whole idea is to blow your mind about a grocery store," says Walter Robb, Co-President and Co-COO of Whole Foods. "This is not your typical grocery store and not your typical shopping experience."[4] He's right: For now, Whole Foods still is kind of a strange grocery store. You can't buy Coke there, but you might stumble into a secret beer cave where a guide lets you sample unusual beers from all over the world in a frosty grotto atmosphere. You can't buy Charmin toilet tissue, but you might be able to learn about 16 types of fresh heirloom eggs in an artistic rainbow of colors—you don't need

---

4 Zimbalist, K. "Green Giant." *Time*, 2006. 167, pp. 24-27.

to buy a whole dozen of one kind, just get one or two of each.

Whole Foods was founded in Austin, Texas, in 1980 by John Mackey as a natural and organic supermarket with a staff of 19. Mackey's management approach is strange—it's been called "equal parts Star Trek and 1970s flashback," and it might have seemed to many like a recipe for failure. But at Whole Foods, this recipe has resulted in amazing growth for a world-changing company.[5] Today, Whole Foods has 181 stores with 40,000 employees and 64 more stores in development, with annual sales of $4.7 billion in 2004. While cooling off some at the time of writing this book (are they losing their strangeness?), same-store sales increased 13% for three years in a row. "Over the past decade, Whole Foods has defined and reshaped the industry," says Edward Aaron, analyst at RBC Capital Markets."[6]

So what type of customer does Whole Paycheck...er, I mean Whole Foods attract? "People who understand why they might not want to eat food with pesticide or why organic might cost more, or who are aware that 90% of American beef contains hormones and what that means," Robb explains.[7] Whole Foods limits itself to areas with college-educated inhabitants, which translates to wealthier neighborhoods and university towns.

How is the workforce strange? What are some of the characteristics and qualities of the Whole Foods workforce that distinguishes the organization from competing groceries? First, they are more likely than average to have some sort of a natural-food obsession and be passionate about sustainable food sources. Universalistic, egalitarian, and liberal values are prevalent. Says one employee, "I just hang on to the fact that my job is good in some larger sense. If people buy the sprouts, they're eating healthier foods, the farmer is doing well, and it's good for the planet because they're grown organically."[8] The goal is to hire employees who maintain that same feeling of mission the original 19 employees felt when they made the decision to work in a little natural-food store. This means that an employee of Whole Foods requires a much higher level of knowledge and passion about food than your average grocery store worker.

[5]   Fishman, C. "The Anarchist's Cookbook." *Fast Company*, 2004: 84, p. 70.

[6]   Zimbalist, K. pp. 24-27.

[7]   Zimbalist, K. pp. 24-27.

[8]   Shapin, S. "Paradise Sold." *New Yorker*, 2006: 82 (13), pp. 84-88.

The staff may seem strange because of the piercings, tattoos, spiky hair, and hemp shoes, and they might also seem strange because of their esoteric knowledge of peach varieties, their willingness to talk about the ingredients of salads, or the virtues of herbal and organic beauty products. As reported in *Fast Company*, here is sample interaction between Aaron Foster—a 22-year old team member whose been with Whole Foods two years—and a customer at the Columbus Circle store who came over from Philadelphia. Foster is a cheese buyer standing at the cheese display:

> *Customer:* "Excuse me. I'm looking for a certain cheese. It begins with a C."
>
> Foster leans forward, all ears.
>
> *Customer:* "It's one syllable. I bought it yesterday at Dean & DeLuca."
>
> *Foster:* "Comte?"
>
> *Customer:* "That's it!" and they head off to get her some.[9]

You, the reader, need to understand something more about Foster and how the Whole Foods workforce is strange. Foster is not just knowledgeable about comte and just about all cheeses; he is passionate about The Quest (notice caps, please). As a cheese buyer, he thinks a lot about things, like— as he puts it—how to "further the goals of sustainable agriculture and artisanal food production while being as big as we are and growing as fast as we are."[10] Is every team member as passionate and knowledgeable about food as Foster? No, of course not. But does the average Whole Foods employee stand out from the average grocery store worker in a way that is noticeable to customers? Yep.

What else is strange and noticeable about the workforce? A high level of focus on food presentation is prevalent because not many items at Whole Foods escape design. "Shopping is 60% impulse, so the more the food is presented in a beautiful and exciting way, that all becomes part of the experience,"[11] Walter Robb explains. This has implications for what the team members in the stores need to deliver. So produce employees are passionate about making the department artful, tearing down and rebuilding their vegetable displays nightly (Hey!

[9]   Fishman, C. p. 70.

[10] Fishman, C. p. 70.

[11] Zimbalist, K. pp. 24-27.

I know! Let's stack the strawberries to resemble those Chinese lanterns in Asian fruit markets!). The prepared-foods employees focus on an expert kebab designer who travels from store to store training team members.

The team members also have to play well with others, since they have lots of decisions to make together, such as who gets a job or what to stock in their stores. Stores are encouraged to buy and stock local produce, fish, and meat, and the regional offices don't dictate what goes on the shelves. In the Austin flagship store, all 600 employees attend monthly meetings: "We talk a lot about choosing our attitudes and what we're going to bring to the table that day," says store team leader Seth Stutzman.[12] Whole Foods stores strive to be "happy stores" with a culture of empowerment and "rule breaking for excellence". The unorthodox idea here is that if you give up some control and allow employees to make mistakes, people get passionate about what they do.

But wait, don't lots of companies want this type of employment setup? It sounds like a great workforce concept for most service establishments. But you can't just hope for this sort of workforce, and it doesn't converge magically. Rather than just talking about this type of workforce, Whole Foods has created some strange design features in its Workforce Architecture to make their Workforce Deliverables more likely to happen. Let's take a look at a caricature of Whole Foods' strange Workforce Architecture.

First, each store makes public the pay of every employee for the previous year. This information is especially valuable if you get promoted or relocated and want to see how your pay stacks up to your colleagues' pay. Think for a little while about what other decisions would need to underpin this one strange design feature, including at a minimum a fair and transparent basis for every pay decision. Speaking of pay, at Whole Foods executive salaries are still limited to 14 times frontline workers' pay. Just in case you don't keep up with the excesses of executive pay in the United States, this compares to about 369-to-1 ratio at other large U.S. companies.[13] CEO John Mackey recently cut his annual salary to $1 with less than a 1% stake in the company.[14] Nonexecutive employees hold 94% of company stock options. Whole

[12] Zimbalist, K. pp. 24-27.

[13] Lublin, J. S. and S. Thurm. "Behind Soaring Executive Pay, Decades of Failed Restraints." *Wall Street Journal*, 2006: Thursday, October 12, p. 1A.

[14] Gray, S. 2006. Natural Competitor. *Wall Street Journal*, December 4, p. B1.

Foods pays 100% of health-insurance costs, and employees vote for the benefits that are most important to them. Full-timers get 20 hours a year of paid time to do volunteer work. This is kind of a big financial commitment when you have 40,000 employees.

What about bringing new people on board—anything strange with Whole Food's hiring decisions? Well, you get hired onto one of about eight functional teams. So, for example, you could be hired by the seafood team, or the prepared-foods team, or the cashier/front-end team. But you are only hired provisionally. After four weeks of work, your team votes you "on or off the island," and you need a two-thirds positive vote to be made a permanent employee. Incentive pay (cash above and beyond base wages) is linked to team productivity, so existing teams are pretty darn careful about who gets voted on the island. Stores also compete against each other in 11 "customer snapshot" reviews a year—on everything from store cleanliness to the drama of the produce displays. Thirteen times a year, Whole Foods looks the performance and productivity of each team in every store. Teams that knocked the cover off the ball get a share of the profits—up to $2.00 extra an hour, every other paycheck. This means that you don't want just anyone on your team; you want workers who are going to make you some money. Do you think these design decisions get employees' attention? Do you think they affect the initial tone of the working relationships?

When opening new stores, the major challenge is not the food—it's ensuring that Whole Foods stays strange and doesn't drift to normal. One practice Whole Foods uses to manage strange is "culturing" new stores with key employees from existing stores, just as if you were culturing a batch of home brew or yogurt. For example, when the Columbus Circle store opened with 292 staff members, 70 came from existing stores. Like pilgrims to a new land, they were the starter culture, launching the fermentation that would turn Columbus Circle into a true Whole Foods store. The two associate store team leaders both ran their own stores in Georgetown and Albuquerque.

The National Leadership Team of the company has 24 people on it and makes decisions by majority vote. At the end of every business meeting at Whole Foods, including the ones that Mackey conducts, is an "appreciations" session—where each participant says something nice about the people in the meeting. Maybe to lots of people this could seem cheesy or corny and like a waste of time. Those people don't work at Whole Foods.

Overall, it kind of seems as if all these strange design decisions are paying off for Whole Foods. First, society is noticing: As you can see from my footnotes, Whole Food's strange people systems are newsworthy and have garnished a lot of free press and free advertising over the years. Whole Foods also has been voted one of Forbes' top 100 companies to work for the past nine years, this year placing fifteenth. You could not buy this type of positive press and advertising, even if you could afford it! And the strange workforce's attitudes, behaviors, and results get noticed by customers and keep them coming back with their wallets. This has produced extraordinary growth and financial results for the company. Adjusting for stock splits and dividends, one share that cost you $2.92 in 1992 would now be worth $62.49. Total revenue last year was more than $5 billion with a gross profit of more than $1.6 billion. In 2004, Whole Foods was "the fastest-growing mass retailer in the U.S." according to the *Financial Times*.[15] Maybe more important to Mackey and the employees, Whole Foods is having a profound impact on how Americans shop and eat.

Should you run out tomorrow and try to copy Whole Food's strange Workforce Architecture? Probably not. Should there be *something* about your Workforce Architecture that is strange? Only if you want a competitive advantage. Or I guess you could try hoping really hard that your normal, ordinary workforce processes will somehow lead to extraordinary results. Good luck with that.

> **Should there be something about your Workforce Architecture that is strange? Only if you want a competitive advantage.**

---

[15] Shapin, S. pp. 84-88.

9

Strange Workforce Architecture: Taking the Next Step

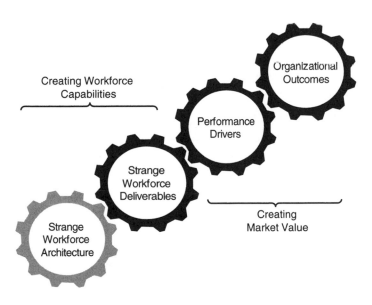

Figure 9.1 Workforce Architecture and your Strange Workforce Value Chain

Once you get a little juiced-up about building a great organization and a strange workforce, here is your four-step plan to help you keep perspective as you move forward with your own strange architecture:

1. **Imagine**. Envision a distinctive people system that can get you to greatness. Don't think of this as "dusting off and freshening up" your existing HR practices. Your thoughts need to be far-reaching and soul-searching—more akin to starting up a new business than renaming your recruitment function or adding dental coverage to your benefits package. Look at the Workforce Deliverables that you developed for a given job (see Chapters 5 and 6). Then using the caricature analogy described in Chapter 8, "Strange Workforce Architecture: Breaking Out From the Pack," ask yourself: "To make it *real* darn likely I will get these deliverables, what about my company do I want to stand out to job seekers and employees? What can I do with my Workforce Architecture so that my company is distinctive and makes people understand early and often what we obsess about in order to win?" Think some big thoughts about how you could really make a big enough splash to gather together and focus a strange, dedicated tribe that customers notice.

2. **Pinpoint gaps**. Once you have a fix on "what could be" in order to be distinctive and successful, then you have a starting place to highlight mismatches between where your Workforce Architecture is now and where it needs to be in order to build a great organization. What you are doing here is highlighting strengths and weaknesses of your existing Workforce Architecture as they relate to achieving your strange Workforce Deliverables. This starts to break the problem into bite-size pieces.

3. **Prioritize**. Determine what strange design elements would have the greatest leverage for getting you to greatness and that are most under your direct control. If you are the CEO, then get ready to makes some serious moves. If you manage a function, you may need to start smaller. For example, one element that may be most within your personal control is exceptional, visible, and frequent performance and feedback discussions that help your people understand and execute strategy. If you feel like you can't affect your organization's policies, then look for elements where you

personally can take your existing systems and strange them up so they feel radically different and work better in your hands than anywhere else in the organization (like weekly team report outs). Look for changes that allow you to fly under the radar of your existing HR system to create a zone of spectacular performance within your suborganization. Other changes to the Workforce Architecture may need to get moved through the formal organizational channels (for example, establishing a scientist career track where the lead scientist earns the kind of money and perks that an EVP gets). These might take longer depending on your leverage in the organization.

4. **Act**. Act as though your business depends on getting the architectural elements in place. Take this as seriously as you take winning. This might mean you evolve the way that you personally invest your time at work so that you become more of a workforce champion and less of an individual contributor. I truly hope so because this type of leader builds great organizations. If at your existing organization you have already established yourself as a "business as usual" kind of manager who is not into workforce issues, by all means find a job somewhere else where you can start fresh and make some things happen. If you really honestly believe that you cannot affect the systems that could make your workforce and your organization great, then what exactly are you leading? Find a more dynamic organization where you can make a difference. Remember, if your workforce is what makes it possible to beat the competition, then the workforce systems that you design are the foundation of your competitive advantage.

Do I Need a Different Workforce Architecture for Different Jobs?

It sure would be nice to create a single strange architecture and use it across your whole organization. A single Workforce Architecture would let you consolidate your design efforts, and would give you the strongest employer brand with a consistent theme and message to all employees (regardless of their roles in the organization). One single architecture also allows for the

most seamless movement of employees between jobs, making lateral assign-
ments and promotions more fluid. Finally, a single architecture doesn't create equity problems between employees.

Unfortunately, it doesn't always work out that way. There are three reasons why it is not always wise to use a single Workforce Architecture across
all your jobs and employees.

Reason #1: Specific Deliverables of Jobs May Require a Different Workforce Architecture

Your Workforce Architecture should reflect and produce whatever customers
find valuable and rare about your people and what competitors find hard to
imitate. For workforce-wide deliverables (the special sauce that is the same
across jobs, described in Chapter 5, "Strange Workforce Deliverables: What
the Workforce Does to Make Customers Notice and Love Us"), everything is
set up nicely for you to use a single Workforce Architecture. But the problem
is that different jobs often need to provide different types of activities and output, and the people in those jobs need to obsess about different things in order
to be successful (we called these "job-specific deliverables" in Chapters 6 and
7). When you need different deliverables from different jobs, then you often
need to have different Workforce Architectures to make that happen.

Coping Strategy

Try to mass customize your strange systems. That is, create a design choice
that makes your firm stand out to employees but then deploy it so that the
same basic architecture focuses on different behaviors or accomplishments
depending on the job. For example, Home Depot could develop and throw lots
of energy into very intensive hiring processes that stand out to applicants and
let Home Depot hire the right strange people across jobs. Perhaps all hires are
evaluated with a drug test a, cognitive ability test, and an interactive exercise.
When hiring service representatives, the interactive exercise involves an angry
customer role play, and the evaluation measure focuses on how well the applicant "talks them down" and builds rapport. When hiring aisle associates in the
plumbing area, the interactive exercise asks applicants to diagnose and fix a
model plumbing system with leaks and problems. As another example of a
mass-customized strange system, you could make all employees' total pay

40% contingent on performance (a strange practice that would get people's attention). But what each employee's pay is contingent *on* depends on the specific job and what must be delivered. Mass customization may allow you to generalize and adapt a single strange architecture across multiple jobs.

Reason #2: Return on Investment May Require Different Architecture

As we have seen many times, creating and measuring a strange Workforce Architecture is very time-consuming and often very expensive. These investments into strange will have far higher returns for jobs that directly execute your strategy. In Chapter 6, "Job-Specific Strangeness: Different Deliverables from Different Jobs," we saw how some jobs are more critical to executing your strategy than others, and we developed a process for isolating these different types of positions in your organization. The upshot was that you should give executor jobs more energy and investment than operator jobs, which, in turn, you should give more than outsourcer jobs.

For example, an obsession on fitness could be called a workforce-wide deliverable for Nike. However, Nike's investments into a strange benefits system (described later in this chapter) might have the highest return in five areas: Strategic Planning, Sales and Customer Service, Research and Development, Marketing, and External Relations. This is where strange employees obsessed on fitness and athletics really differentiate Nike to customers and the public at large. These functions are why Nike might invest so much into strange benefits and rewards in the first place. Nike's return on investment into their strange benefits might be lower (but still positive) for Information Technology, Internal Communications, and Human Resources. Fitness obsession still matters for these functions because when they share core values with the public-facing employees who they serve, communication and trust increase.[1] But perhaps these internal-facing roles are not why Nike would set up the strange benefits in the first place. There may be other roles where the return on investment into attracting and retaining employees with a fitness obsession is lowest—for example, Supply Chain or Finance.

---

[1] Cable, D. M. & Edwards, J. R. (2006). "The value of value congruence." Paper presented at the National Academy of Management Annual Meeting, Atlanta, Georgia.

Coping Strategy

If there are strange design elements of your Workforce Architecture that you can set up primarily for your executor positions and then apply to all positions at basically the same cost, it makes sense to just do it. For example, once Nike invests in amazing fitness centers, it likely costs little additional resources to extend the plan to all employees. Likewise, once Lincoln Electric commits to giving 30% of profits back to employees, it might make sense to extend this element to all employees, from Manufacturing to Legal, since it allows Lincoln to pay less fixed salary while creating a culture of solidarity and a focus on the bottom line. However, if there are very high costs incurred for each additional employee covered by a strange design decision, then you must consider your return on investment into strange, and create a different Workforce Architecture for your executor positions.

Returning to the example of the wood delivery company that depends on truck drivers to develop strong ties with clients and gather information about upcoming shipments, it may make sense for them to invest a full day evaluating truck drivers. The hiring system could be radically different from what truckers are expecting—to get their attention and to increase the odds of hiring a strange workforce. So in addition to facing a difficult obstacle course where driving abilities are graded, the hiring system could include a priorities and values computer test, a panel interview conducted by three of the best existing drivers, role-play exercises with angry "clients" to see how they cope with interaction stress, and taking them on-site to meet the primary clients and having the clients evaluate them. Forklift drivers, on the other hand, might be hired with a three-hour selection process, including reading a loading order and detecting "errors" in math on the order, operating a forklift and loading a truck safely and accurately, and panel interviews with the best existing loaders. Both are far stranger systems than the trucker and loader applicants would receive at most any other company in the world, but higher investments into the driver position are based on the more critical role of the position to the company's ability to differentiate.

Reason #3: Structure of Jobs May Require Different Architecture

Some jobs have to be treated with different systems because the process and outcomes of the work itself are so different between jobs. For example, why is it that pay for sales jobs is traditionally much more contingent on performance than other types of jobs? Because sales work is generally more entrepreneurial, individualistic, and less programmed than other jobs. Because the results of sales work is more measurable than many other jobs, and the specific value added to the company can be calculated in a more direct way. In the same vein, Lincoln Electric relies on piece-rate incentives for its manufacturing positions in a way that differentiates the company and affects the type of people who work there. When I asked Roy Morrow, the Director of Corporate Relations at Lincoln Electric, whether he was under a piece-rate plan, he said "No, I don't get paid by the word." The fact is that Roy's work is not as programmed, and the results are less immediately countable than manufacturing work. For this reason, Lincoln has to use a different pay structure for leadership positions.

Coping Strategy

Craft your strange design decisions and build your Workforce Architecture around your executor positions. Make sure, first and foremost, that you are creating an executor workforce that differentiates your organization from the competition. Then, try like heck to stretch and pull your strange architecture to also cover the non-executor positions as much as possible and see where it tears and breaks down. For non-executor roles, you may need to dilute the strange system to make it work, while trying to preserve the essential nature of the design decisions. For example, while Lincoln Electric cannot use a piece-rate incentive system for leadership positions, much more of leaders' pay is contingent on company profitability. That is, an equivalent percentage of leaders' pay is linked to performance just like the factory workers, but the risk is based on company profitability rather than daily production.

Make It Simple, Stupid

Q: Do I need to create and use strange, noticeable people systems for my *executor* positions?

A: Absolutely positively, unless you think that your strange workforce will occur by chance or hope. Executor positions are what you start imagining and designing your strange Workforce Architecture around because this is where strange matters most.

Q: Do I need to use strange, noticeable people systems for my *operator* positions?

A: This is more difficult to answer because it depends. There may be places where you can apply some of your strange systems to operator positions, but you might need to adapt, dilute, and invest less into the strange architecture for these roles.

Q: Do I need to use strange, noticeable people systems for my *outsourcer* positions?

A: We don't call them outsourcers for nothing! This is where you should be spending the least energy and resources to be strange. Push this work outside your organization if possible (so that the outsource organization can worry about being strange and creating workforce obsession for this stuff). For employer branding and consistency reasons, it makes sense be strange for outsourcer roles when the architecture is already set up for the executor roles and when it doesn't cost you to extend the strange treatment to the entire organization.

Build in Measurement

Most organizations say they pay for performance, but they don't (the difference between the smallest and largest raise is often less than 3%). Most organizations say they pay above the market in order to attract and retain the best and the brightest, but statistically it is impossible for most organizations to pay above average. Most organizations say that they hire based on fit with the organizational culture, but what they really mean is, "I liked him." You get the picture: Talk is cheap. Many of the organizations making these claims about their Workforce Architecture do not have evidence to support them and in fact are fooling themselves.

Measuring your Workforce Architecture ideas forces you to crystallize fuzzy concepts and gets people to agree about what the concepts really look like in the real world. Measuring your ideas allows you to test whether, in real terms, you are getting a bang for your buck or just throwing away money. In Chapter 2, "Shine a Flashlight into the Black Box That Exists Between Your Workforce and Beating Your Competition," I referred to measurements of your Workforce Architecture as *mapping indicators* because they let you see if you are actually on the route you mapped out. Measuring lets you demonstrate to yourself that you have pulled the levers to steer your competitive advantage.

For example, you may be proud of your forced-ranking performance evaluations that let you fire the worst 5% of employees every year. This system definitely has the attention of employees. However, unless you have data showing that your best employees perceive the system—and your organization—as fair and performance-oriented, then you may not actually be getting the value out of the system that you think you are. It's important to know and not just hope.

Improve your thinking and execution of your architecture design decisions by deciding how you will collect data. For each strange design decision, first describe the concept verbally (how would the design look and feel—from your perspective and from the perspective of those affected by it). Then develop measures that will tell you when you have set up the system in the intended way. The measurement comes in two varieties: activities and results. That is, you can measure the activities that your organization will engage in to create the strange architecture, and you can measure how your targeted job seekers and employees should view the strange architecture once you set it up right.

Just Do It (and Then Just Measure It)

With the mission of being the #1 sports and fitness company, Nike strives to differentiate itself by selling its customers a whole fitness experience. From this perspective, I can think of several good reasons for Nike to prefer physically fit employees who obsess about fitness and being healthy over employees who are out of shape and unhealthy. For starters, consider (a) the brand image that is conveyed to customers by every Nike employee in both professional and personal settings, (b) the ability for a fitness-oriented workforce to understand and innovate toward athletes' needs, and (c) employee health care costs.

Problem: How could Nike create a strange benefits and rewards system that attracts the type of people they value most?

Solution: In addition to providing a world-class, state-of-the-art exercise facility and health club to employees and their families, what if Nike paid employees (through credits they earn) to *use* it daily? What if Nike also paid employees bonuses to participate in on-site annual physical exams, to not be overweight, and to not smoke? What if Nike gave employees 50% off anything the company produces? To create time for employees and help them balance their lives, what if Nike partnered with Whole Foods to offer discounted healthy staples that employees could order online with free delivery to them at work? What if Nike allowed employees to bank their sick time so that after ten years, healthy employees could receive up to five weeks of paid sabbatical time to recharge?[2] To people who love to exercise and being healthy, these design decisions—and the subsequent workforce culture it inculcates—would be extremely attractive. To employees who were physically unhealthy, they would be worthless or perhaps aversive.

What activities and results could Nike measure to ensure that the benefits package was set up and working as intended? Nike could survey new employees to learn what benefits they received and appreciated at their last organization compared to what they received at Nike to learn whether they were indeed extraordinary in the right areas and whether new employees said, "Wow!" Nike also could track the usage rates of the benefits (gym use, Whole Foods orders, etc.), and could examine whether the best employees used the benefits more or less than other employees. In terms of results, Nike

---

[2] 1995. Nike pushes the limits with LifeTrek. Compensation and Benefits Review, January-February: 74–76.

could ask job applicants on an online application or during the interview process which Nike benefits they know about and which sounded most interesting to them. Nike could also examine the percentage of times employees write in the various benefits on a survey when asked what benefits they find most valuable.

Sounds like a lot of work, doesn't it? Why spend time collecting this data? Isn't this just a paper chase? It depends on whether or not this is truly one of the two or three most important determinants of creating your strange workforce. If your benefits program is just table stakes—that is, serviceable and unexceptional—then it likely is not worth gathering extraordinary data. But if benefits are how you plan to differentiate your organization to employees and job applicants and are a cornerstone of building your strange workforce, then it is not a paper chase. It is the source of your competitive advantage. In this latter case, you collect the data (a) because it puts teeth rather than just hope into your ideas of winning and lets you know that you are working toward your strategy and (b) you can learn whether the system is having its intended results or whether you were dreaming expensive dreams. If you don't measure your most important systems, you start to cut corners when the going gets tough. You start to trim benefits to make profitability estimates or skip the measurement and just, "get through the people stuff as quickly as possible so that you can get back to real work." You start to become normal rather than valuable, unique, and hard to imitate. By measuring and testing the genesis of your strange workforce, you are becoming a management scientist making fact-based decisions about your resources and your competitive advantage through people.

That's why the next chapter of the book is dedicated to the magic of measurement and metrics.

10

The Magic of Metrics: Creating and Implementing Measurement Systems

This chapter is *very* important. I wanted to make this the second chapter of the book, but if I had, I ran the risk of your putting the book down and walking away from it—because measuring fuzzy stuff is hard and annoying. But the cold, hard fact is that collecting *valid* data on the *right* concepts is what makes a lot of the ideas in this book valuable. If you don't put any discipline into your concepts, then the link between strategizing and doing gets tenuous. When the going gets tough and you get busy, it will be hard to be strange without discipline because strange demands a lot more energy than just being like everyone else.

Why are metrics so helpful in directing workforce behavior? I think it's because human beings share an interesting relationship with metrics—that is, counting things. Metrics are sort of magical. When you tell people what will be counted and scored, they focus on those things *a lot*—often to the exclusion of other things going on in the environment.

Want some proof? Daniel Simons at the University of Illinois created a video of people passing basketballs to each other, some wearing black shirts and some wearing white shirts.[1] When you tell people to watch the video and count the number of passes made by the team wearing white, most people literally do not "see" a large hairy gorilla walk right through the middle of the group passing the ball around. Why? Because they are too focused on counting the ball passes by the team wearing white. The human mind somehow blocks out stimuli that was not supposed to be counted. They tune out the gorilla because it has become irrelevant.[2] What is counted can change the reality that humans experience. And this is just a little lab experiment with no career, promotions, or incentives on the line to really heighten people's focus on the metric. Simply providing and emphasizing a metric is generally enough to get individuals to focus on it and ignore other seemingly obvious information.

Important leadership implication: Metrics can help your organization get strange because metrics instruct people what to obsess about. What you measure gets people's attention. What you don't measure gets neglected.[3] People in your workforce will change their focus and their behaviors depending on what gets measured.

> **Your metrics need to be focused on what you and your workforce *should* be obsessing about instead of focused on what is easy to measure.**

Corollary: Odds are good that you are going to get attention around what you measure, even if it is not what you really want. Your metrics need to be focused on what you and your workforce *should* be obsessing about instead of focused on what is easy to measure.

---

[1] You can go try this yourself at http://viscog.beckman.uiuc.edu/grafs/demos/15.html. If you seriously try to count just the number of passes made by the white team, your mind *still* will try to block out the gorilla even after reading about the gorilla!

[2] Simons, D. J., & Chabris, C. F. "Gorillas in Our Midst: Sustained Inattentional Blindness for Dynamic Events." *Perception*, 1999: 28, pp. 1059-1074; also see Simons, D. J. "Attentional Capture and Inattentional Blindness." *Trends in Cognitive Sciences,* 2000: 4, pp. 147-155.

[3] Craig, C. E., & Harris, R.C. "Total Productivity Measurement at the Firm Level." *Sloan Management Review*, 1973: 14, 13-28.

Strapping Numbers onto Fuzzy Concepts

What *is* a metric? When you really get down to it, metrics strap numbers onto concepts that you can't see in the real world. It's one thing to measure crown molding, where you can get your trusty tape measure and strap a number onto a concept called "length." It's another thing altogether to measure a job seeker's intelligence because you just can't see or touch intelligence. I mean, we all think that intelligence *exists*, and we all want to hire intelligent people, but it's hard to know what it really *is*. It's hard to strap numbers onto it. Throughout this book, I described metrics as a critical tool for building a Strange Workforce and a great organization. But I also hinted at the special hell that you need to endure to measure your competitiveness concepts in a valid way. This chapter deals with how to get through it successfully.

Are Performance Metrics a Fad?

Nowadays lots of managers are told by their bosses that they need to "come up with some metrics" or to "develop a balanced scorecard." Often the bosses don't really know what they are asking for, or maybe they just want metrics because their boss told *them* to come up with some metrics. In any case, many managers charged with creating a balanced scorecard are not equipped to understand what to measure, how to pick the right metrics, or how to actually obtain the data. So what seems to happen often is they either take something that is already being measured and relabel it, or they grab some stuff that can be measured pretty easily and then hand it in dutifully as a balanced scorecard. This balanced scorecard initiative begins to drive some wrong workforce behaviors because the metrics don't line up with how value is actually created for customers. Leaders don't really use the data. Everyone involved gets frustrated with balanced scorecards, and whole initiative gets swept under the rug to rot away, and everybody hopes it will just disappear and not stink too much.

Just because metrics are hard doesn't mean that they don't work. To the contrary, it is *because* metrics are potent but difficult that they have the power to be part of your competitive advantage. If you set them up right so that they reflect the core of how you differentiate and create value as an organization,

> **Just because metrics are hard doesn't mean that they don't work.**

metrics bring discipline and focus that help you to execute your strategy (while your competitors are talking and wishing). You just can't expect metrics to be easy or quick. The point of this book is to give you a framework for understanding what to measure in order to build a strange workforce and win. The point of this chapter is to give some background for understanding the process, pitfalls, and power of developing metrics.

Metrics Koan

Ever heard of a koan? A koan is a puzzling, or even paradoxical set of statements used by Zen Buddhists as an aid to meditation and a means of gaining spiritual awakening. It may sound a little heavy in a business setting, but I think that you need your very own koan when whenever you are developing and deploying metrics. The metrics koan asks you to hold two very different thoughts in your head simultaneously.

I need to use metrics to build a great organization.

This particular metric may be more trouble than it's worth.

Figure 10.1   The metrics koan

The goal of this koan is to help to keep you awake (in the intellectual sense) as you develop and implement your metrics. Both statements are true, but they are difficult to hold in your head at once because they seem incompatible. Why is it valuable to hold both thoughts in your head at once? Here are two reasons:

Developing Metrics

When developing measures for your strategic concepts, your *attitude* toward the process matters a lot. **On the one hand**, you need to be sensitive to how powerful and important metrics are and how they are needed to build a strange workforce, which is the basis of a great organization. You need to be committed to metrics so that you work very diligently and seriously to best represent your concepts with numbers. **On the other hand**, you must also be awake to the fact that no metric is a perfect representation of your concepts. Soon after developing a metric and gathering data, you and your workforce will likely spot flaws in the metric. You will identify slippage and slop in your measurement once you start using it. So while you must be committed to the *process* of measuring things, you need to stay flexible and not grow over-attached to any *one* particular metric (even though you worked hard at developing it). You will need to modify, update, and correct your metrics across time as you discover flaws.

By the way, if it helps out at all, there is a silver lining when you discover flaws in a metric you worked hard on: You learn something important about executing your strategy. In Chapter 6, "Job-Specific Strangeness: Different Deliverables from Different Jobs," we called this process "grounding your strategy." It is only through the discipline that a metric brought to your thinking and behavior that you discovered why the metric was not accurate in capturing what you really intended with your strategy. When you try to measure your concepts and you learn how your thinking was flawed, you learn about your customers, competitors, and workforce behaviors. If you are confident that you must measure your strange concepts to build a great organization, then the demise of any one metric will result in strategic learning, better metrics, and more winning. The koan helps you become a flexible metrics artist rather than someone who jumps on the metrics bandwagon only to discover that "metrics don't work" and then jump back off into mediocrity.

Implementing Metrics

When you introduce a system of metrics to your workforce, your presentation of and stance toward the metrics matter a lot. **On the one hand**, you need to make your workforce understand that you made a serious investment to measure the right things and that you currently think it is the best representation of the unique way that your organization needs to win. **On the other hand**, you need to convey to your workforce that the proposed metrics are not forever. Your workforce needs to grasp intellectually and emotionally that this particular set of metrics is not a permanent "solution," but a tactic that will focus everyone on the best things you know until the organization learns better ways to represent what you really mean by winning. The workforce must be willing to tell you and other leaders when the metrics backfire and cause unintended consequences. Employees must be willing to offer advice about how and why the proposed metrics are not a good reflection of winning. This is an integral part of how you will improve the metrics and learn more about competing. If you present your metrics as "the final solution," then two very negative things occur:

- **Disengagement.** Your workforce will be much less likely to point out limitations and offer improvements to the metrics, even though they certainly have ideas about them.

- **Cynicism.** When you must eventually change your system of metrics, the workforce will view you as erratic and will view subsequent metrics as a "flash in the pan" or a "flavor of the month" that will also pass if they just wait you out.

F. Scott Fitzgerald wrote that "The test of a first-rate intelligence is the ability to hold two opposed ideas in the mind at the same time and still retain the ability to function." The metrics koan helps you keep the right attitude toward metrics in your own mind, which is necessary in order for you to develop valid metrics and communicate them to your workforce. Metrics are not something that you "solve" and then get back to business.

How Do I Get the Right Metrics?

Make yourself a list: "Here is the list of concepts that we talk about as being vital to winning but that we do not measure well." This list represents your strategic liabilities. It's like having a crystal ball telling you the parts of your strategy that are not likely to be executed successfully.

So what we need to do is take this list of strategic concepts that you can't see or touch—but that you think are really important to winning—and convert them into numbers that you can gather and manage. There are four steps in this process:

1. Get your theory straight.
2. Define your competitiveness concepts.
3. Develop measures of your competitiveness concepts.
4. Put the data into a spreadsheet.

Let's first work through a hypothetical example and then use it to describe how the four-step process works. Your job will then be to take this process of metrics creation and apply it to your own organization following the Strange Workforce Value Chain described in Chapters 3 through 9.

Clean Competition

You operate a chain of 36 family restaurants in the Southeast. Your competitive advantage rests on a wholesome family image, affordable value meals, and good central locations near family shopping destinations. One element of your workforce strategy has been hiring servers and wait staff (the face of your restaurant) who are exceptionally courteous and polite, who like talking to kids, and who portray a clean-cut image.

After encountering some declines in same-store sales in several areas, you run some focus groups and learn that many potential customers perceive your restaurants as dirty. The perception of dirty restaurants may be corroding your image and turning off customers. You do currently track restaurant cleanliness as your Sanitation Grade, which is really not that bad (your average score across restaurants is an 89.5, with a range from 87 to 92) and is not trending downward even in the worst-performing restaurants.

You want to develop a measure of the concept "restaurant cleanliness" for each restaurant each month. What are your measurement options? One approach is activity-based—you could use the employee cleaning schedules that you already have (when and how often were the bathrooms cleaned, the floors mopped, the counters wiped). This approach might seem attractive because some of the data are already being collected and wouldn't be too hard to formalize, and it could be managed easily (start cleaning more often). Unfortunately, the data might not tell you too much about the flavor of cleanliness you care about. The strategic concept you're interested in is *customers' perceptions* of cleanliness, and these perceptions may not be captured by your activities (for example how many times you mopped the bathrooms).

What's another measurement option? How about hiring mystery shoppers to periodically "shop the restaurants" by eating a meal and then completing a survey about the experience, including cleanliness of the service counter, tables, and bathrooms? This option also would allow you to get ratings of service levels, particularly politeness and interactions with kids. Although mystery shoppers would be more expensive, it would give you an "objective" or "outsider" perspective on restaurant cleanliness, service, and food preparation. This might be a solid option for some valid data.

What about asking the customers themselves? This is probably the worst idea if done incorrectly and the best idea if done right. The problem is that there are many ways to do it wrong and only a few ways to do it right. For example, putting surveys out on the tables probably would be ignored by customers or might become toys for bored teenagers. You might get a few surveys back in a month, but the response rate might be low, and the data might not be valid or representative. You probably don't want to make business decisions based on this data.

What's a right way to ask customers? Maybe every 100th customer is invited to complete a two-minute survey about their dining experience for a $10 gift certificate. Sounds like a good start, but who could you really rely on to present the survey and gift certificate to customers in a compelling, interesting way? You might want to invest in training and role playing wait staff or perhaps cashiers on how to distribute and present the survey and the gift certificate. Although this customer survey would probably be less comprehensive than the mystery shopper survey, it could still hit your core competitiveness concepts. It would yield some solid data if you could get a good percentage of those approached to complete the survey, and the gift certificate would likely drive some repeat business. This may be a positive investment given its synergies with your competitive advantage because the survey training and role playing might get the workforce involved in a way that "overflows" onto how employees treat customers in general.

Or maybe restaurant managers should be the ones who invite every 100th customer to participate and hand over the gift certificate when the customer completes the survey. This likely would improve both the response rate and the quality of the data, and it would have the side effect of getting the managers out and talking to the customers and learning from them.

So now let's use this restaurant example to dig into the four general steps of developing metrics:

1. **Get your theory straight.** I hope you're not the type who scoffs when people say, "There is nothing as practical as a good theory." A theory is practical because it tells you what to pay attention to. So before you can decide what to measure, you need to start with a clear story about what causes your customers to notice and like your organization. This is your theory of winning, and you are developing one whenever you create a business plan or develop an organizational change. The Strange Workforce Value Chain presented in this book is how you develop your theory of winning through your people.

    To get your story straight, try to break your theory of winning into "if-then" statements. For the "clean restaurants" example, you could develop two initiatives, executing one approach in 18 restaurants and the other approach in the other 18 restaurants. The "if-then" statements might look something like these:

    Initiative I (18 restaurants)

    -   If we train restaurant employees on cleaning expectations and what the store should look like at all times, they will keep the restaurants cleaner.

    -   If employees keep the restaurants cleaner, customers will notice and evaluate the restaurants as cleaner.

Initiative II (18 restaurants)

- If we repaint and install new flooring in the restaurants, customers will evaluate the restaurants as cleaner.

All 36 restaurants

- If customers evaluate our restaurants as more clean and attractive, then our image will improve, and customers will be more likely to choose us again (repeat business).

- If our servers and wait staff are evaluated as more courteous, polite, and kid-focused, then our image will be stronger, and customers will be more likely to choose us again (repeat business).

This restaurant initiative is just a small example illustrating the type of thinking that goes into a single strategic measure. But the process of developing and testing your entire Strange Workforce Value Chain is basically the same, although larger in scope. All your if-then statements add up to your theory of winning. It should be compelling, easy to explain, and should show why and how you will beat competitors and win customers. Your theory of winning is the core of everything you measure.

2. **Define your competitiveness concepts.** Your if-then statements specify your organization's unique way of operating and what will be strange about your organization and your workforce. Your competitiveness concepts are the key factors you are trying to manage in order to make customers notice you. Some examples of competitiveness concepts from the restaurant's if-then statements might include "successful training," "store cleanliness," "courtesy," "kid-focus," and "repeat business."

Your goal is to be really clear about the movable parts of your competitiveness story, the parts that you have some ability to influence and change in order to add unique value to your customers and dominate your competitors. You and your leadership team need to refine your understanding of your competitiveness concepts and describe how they fit together and affect each other to the point where you are ready to try to capture them and attach numbers to them.

In the restaurant example, the concept "successful training" might be defined as follows:

A successful training session is one in which the employees rate themselves as knowledgeable about our expectations around cleanliness and appearance in the restaurant. A successfully trained employee can walk through the restaurant and identify items that are not up to our standards (garbage or crayons in the aisles, tables not bussed and wiped, windows streaked or dusty). A successfully trained employee can explain back to us why clean stores help us to win.

3. **Develop valid measures of your concepts.** Once you have your competitiveness concepts defined and arranged so you know what causes what, you need to come up with an approach to collect some actual data about each of the concepts. Our goal here is to develop measures that maximize validity—where validity refers to how truly the data map onto your concept. Naturally, you also want measures that minimize effort and cost, but honestly if your *primary* goal is to minimize effort and cost, then this metrics process is not worth pursuing.

   Developing a valid measurement approach for a concept is probably the hardest step in the process. I think that it's so hard because something close to alchemy is going on during this step. This is the point where you are taking words and changing them into numbers. I think every business owner or leader should get excited about this—you are taking fuzzy ideas about winning and differentiating, and you are translating them into something disciplined that can be tracked and analyzed and managed. This is your business and the way you will win or lose.

   The way that you go about gathering the data will affect the validity of the data, which affects your ability to trust and use the data. This is a garbage-in/garbage-out situation. You may need to fight the temptation to represent your concepts using data that are already being collected for something else. Remember that the data must reflect your particular competitiveness concept, or the data will not have the ability to create any unique value. There is generally a reverse relationship between the ease of collecting data and the value of the data for tracking your unique strategy.

Measuring the wrong thing cheaply means that you won't use the data to make decisions anyway, and no value will be created. Cheap metrics still have a terrible return on investment if they can't help you make decisions. Even worse, cheap, invalid metric cause people to act in ways that are *contrary* to winning. Your first priority—measure the right thing. Your second priority—measure the right thing as efficiently as possible.

> **Your first priority—measure the right thing. Your second priority—measure the right thing as efficiently as possible.**

Another common metrics problem is trying to measure everything. When you measure everything, you probably don't represent anything very well, and you probably don't use much of the data. It would be far better to stop investing the energy measuring everything poorly and put the energy into measuring the few right things. This is when a theory becomes so darn useful. The right things to measure are the competitiveness concepts in your theory of differentiating and winning, and the intent of the Strange Workforce Value Chain is to help you identify them for your organization. A major goal of this book is to try to get you to focus on developing valid measures of the right things—the important things—and let go of your other measures. Investing your energy and resources into only measuring the few right things allows you to prioritize, which makes you and your workforce obsess about the right things and gives you the discipline to execute your strategy.

For each competitiveness concept, make it a point to figure out at least one or two measures—valid measures —of that concept. Ask of each competitiveness concept: "What would the world look like if we did that?" and "How could we prove to an objective observer that we did that?" To learn about restaurant cleanliness and its effects on business, for example, you might triangulate restaurant sanitation grade, a monthly mystery shopper score, and the customer surveys to provide complementary insights (because each metric offers a different perspective on clean restaurants).

4. **Put the data into a spreadsheet.** The ultimate goal is to use your data to make decisions. Create a spreadsheet where the columns are your concepts (for example, "customer-rated cleanliness" might be a column of data

that represents one restaurant's cleanliness, as rated by customers). It may be useful if the rows represent some meaningful time increment of how often you're going to collect the data (week, month, quarter, year).

If all you do is input and track your competitiveness concepts, it is valuable because this brings discipline to your theory of winning, and you gain an understanding of whether you are achieving your special sauce. But you can go farther with the data. After you gather enough data in a spreadsheet, a golden grail may beckon you: You may be able to *test* your theory and the linkages between your concepts if your sample of data is large enough. For example, after gathering and inputting the data a few months in the restaurant example, you could learn which are the dirtiest and cleanest restaurants according to the different measures. You could examine the restaurants where the variance is the greatest between the measures, visit those restaurants, and try to see which measures seem most valid and why. You could run regression analyses to see which of the measures best predicts overall restaurant reputation, repeat visits, and financial results. You could examine whether the investments into better lighting and flooring is more or less effective than the investments into training employees, in terms of affecting customers' cleanliness perceptions, restaurant image, and financial results. You can make data-based management decisions.

Who's Afraid of Measurement Error?

Whenever you measure something, measurement error rears its ugly head. Measurement error is the part of your data that is *not* tied to the concept that you care about. For example, once upon a time scientists measured the concept of intelligence by measuring the size of the skull.[4] (It makes some sense, right? If the brain is where intelligence lives, then a bigger brain means more intelligence, and it would need a bigger home.) But that method of measuring intelligence didn't turn out to be valid. Nowadays, we use standardized tests like the Scholastic Aptitude Test (SAT) as a way to strap

---

[4] Stephen Jay Gould. 1981. *The Mismeasure of Man*. New York. Norton.

numbers on the intelligence concept. Does an SAT score *really* capture everything we mean by the concept of intelligence? What about street smarts, emotional intelligence (EQ), or mechanical aptitude? Let's face it: an SAT score is not a perfect approximation of a person's intelligence. We know that there is slippage—the SAT misses lots of what we mean when we talk about intelligence.

What about our restaurant example? Let's say that you have a column of data under the title "customer-rated cleanliness" sitting there in your spreadsheet. You worked really hard to get the data—your store managers are out talking with customers and getting them to do the surveys; you're giving out the $10 certificates; and you have about 40% of the invited customers completing the surveys. But is the data a perfect reflection of the concept "restaurant cleanliness?" No, there are lots of possible slippage points between the concept and the data. For example, the 40% of the people completing your surveys may be different from the 60% of the people who do not complete the surveys. Different respondents might attach different meaning to the cleanliness question based on their expectations and past restaurant experiences. Some might be harsher judges of cleanliness, and some might be lenient judges. Let's face it—there is error in your measure of restaurant cleanliness.

The right question is not whether there *is* error in your measure—the right question is whether there is more usable truth or misleading error in your measure. A measurement is not going to be perfect—ever. What you need to ask is whether the data you collected is a close enough approximation of reality to be useful in making management decisions. Can it make you better at managing a concept than your competition? Despite measurement error, universities' admissions offices use standardized intelligence tests like the SAT as one part of their decision about who is more likely to excel in their program and in life because it is more predictive of success than randomly admitting people.

How do you know if you have enough validity in your measure to make it worth using? Now *that's* a good question. There is not a formula to answer the question because it's a judgment call based on several factors. Let's look at three litmus tests you can think about using:

- First, take a very close look at some of the high points and the low points in the data you collect on a concept. Do these minimum and maximum data map onto real life in a usable way? In the restaurant example, are there things that managers of restaurants rated lowest in cleanliness can learn from managers of restaurants rated highest in cleanliness? Can managers improve their cleanliness scores by working harder at it?

- Second, do your data predict anything that you care about? Based on your theory, what competitiveness concepts that you measure should be moving up or down together (co-variation). In the restaurant example, across your 36 restaurants is there a correlation between perceived cleanliness scores and sanitation grades? More important, is there a correlation between restaurants' perceived cleanliness scores and customer repeat business?

- Third, sit down and talk to your best employees who can affect (and who are affected by) your metric. Ask them: "Do these numbers help us figure out how to be better? Are any high performers being hurt by these measures and why? How are poor performers gaming these measures?"

Despite all the work you have put into developing a measure and collecting some data, odds are that you probably won't get it perfectly right the first time. Remember the metrics koan: You need to stay open to the possibility that the particular method you are using to collect data about a competitiveness concept will reveal flaws once you start using it. This does not mean you should drop the measurement idea, sweep it under the rug, and start winging it. If this really is a concept that helps you win or will make you lose, capturing it with a valid measure is not a "nice to have"—it is how you bring discipline to your theory of winning, execute your strategy, and out-perform competitors. You either need to find another method of collecting the data, or you need to find a different concept to give you a competitive advantage.

Antagonistic Concepts: Get the Balance Right

In Chapter 3, "Organizational Outcomes: How Do I Know I Am Winning in the Way I Want to Win?," we discussed the concept of antagonistic measures— choosing *families* of competing metrics that together keep the organization focused on the right things, rather than maximizing any one incomplete success metric. Whenever you measure a concept, organizational activity shifts toward that concept. This is a Goldilocks phenomenon: A little additional focus on the concept is a good thing, but too much additional focus on a single concept creates suboptimization that hurts your organization. If a given metric focuses your workforce too much on it, they may not see the gorilla in the middle of the room.

Or, worse yet, your workforce may *see* the gorilla but intentionally ignore it because employees are "gaming" your metric. Gaming is a special, evil class of suboptimization. Unfortunately, metrics and gaming go hand-in-hand. You create a problem whenever you choose a metric, place it out there for your workforce, point to it and say, "This is how we will define success." The problem is that you just might get what you asked for—and *only* get what you asked for. Lots of other behaviors and results that you were accustomed to getting from your workforce vanish because they are not part of your measure. For example, if you are a cell phone manufacturer having trouble meeting product launch deadlines, you might develop good metrics around launch deadlines and the activities that precede an on-time launch. The engineering group makes sure they hit the launch deadlines, mostly by cutting corners in the design, documentation, and test phases of production. These new behaviors, while accomplishing the launch deadline goals, lead to manufacturing and design flaws once the product is shipping as well as an inability for other teams to understand or improve on the design. Is this a metrics success story? Well, you've managed the workforce's behavior, just not in a way that makes customers want to give you their money. Examples like this help show why it is important to choose three to four antagonistic metrics that work as a family to represent true long-term value creation.

Summary

Figure 10.2 summarizes the points made in this chapter and might serve as a guide as you convert your theory of winning into data that you use to execute your strategy. Here's how to interpret the figure to get the important take-aways:

1. Make sure you can articulate your theory of how you will differentiate from and beat your competition. This is the center of everything you measure, as shown in the figure.

2. Formalize your competitiveness concepts and map out how they affect each other. This is what the Strange Workforce Value Chain helps you figure out. This is the meaning of the arrows between the concepts (concept B causes concept A to occur).

3. Figure out what concepts are most critical. Don't measure everything, just what few competitive concepts are most important to differentiating and are reflective of winning.

4. Make sure that the competitive concepts antagonize each other so that as a system they prove that you are winning and not just temporarily gaming a metric in isolation. This is the meaning of the lightning bolts in the figure.

5. Develop approaches to collecting data that actually represent your concepts so that the data are meaningful and useful and not just measurement error. It may be useful to develop multiple measures of key concepts so that you can triangulate your data.

6. Put the data into a spreadsheet on an on-going basis so that you can bring discipline to your concepts and know whether you are managing successfully and perhaps even test the links between the concepts.

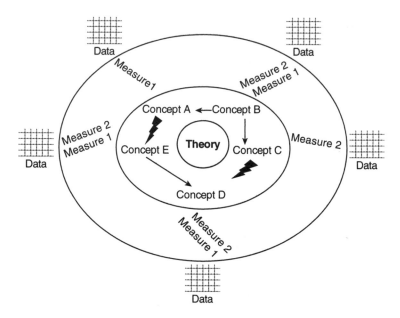

Figure 10.2 Converting ideas into data

Conclusion

Let's wrap up this book where we started. Here is the basic logic that gets you to strange: Your organization is not going to be great unless your customers reliably notice something out of the ordinary about your products and services. And customers are probably not going to detect much extraordinary about your products and services if your workforce is essentially the same as your competitors'. This is why it is advantageous to make the change to strange.

Making the change to strange is a lot of hard work, and it also can be risky. We covered many reasons why the attempt to become extraordinary can fail. This is the reason most of the organizations within an industry are interchangeable from a customer perspective. The good news is that there are solid opportunities for competitive advantage in this area because most organizations are not very strategic or thoughtful about differentiating through their people or their people management systems. In fact, most organizations chase "benchmark averages" for their people systems and rush to be just like everyone else (only cheaper). Most organizations are not particularly good at linking their workforce metrics to their ability to make customers say, "Wow!" or put the hurtin' on competitors.

At a minimum, I hope this book convinced you to stop hoping for extraordinary results with an ordinary, normal workforce. Extraordinary results don't show up by magic; they show up when you build a workforce that is willing and able to convert your ideas about differentiating and winning into a reality that customers notice and embrace.

This book wins if you use the *Strange Workforce Value Chain* to develop your story about your workforce and how they are going to make customers want to give you their business and tell their friends about you. This book knocks the cover off the ball if it helps you develop measures that allow you to manage whether your workforce is helping you make your story come true. And this book puts you in another game entirely if you use this data to make results-based decisions about your investments into building a strange workforce and a great organization.

Index

A

Aaron, Edward, 137
ability, in gaming approach, 65
accomplishment-based workforce
    deliverables, 98-99
actions-based workforce
    deliverables, 99-100
  fine lines in, 104-105
  Home Depot example, 105-106
  Novant Health example,
    100-102

airplane engine mechanics
    example, 2-4, 132-136
antagonistic metrics, 49, 170
architecture. *See* Strange
    Workforce Architecture
articulating strategy, 18-19

B

bank example, 84
  testing strategy, 20-22
bank teller example, 102-104
baseball example, 73-75, 78-79

Stuck in the middle of your career and looking for great meaning and greater impact? Then Vince Thompson's *Ignited: Managers! Light Up Your Company and Career for More Power More Purpose and More Success* is the book for you.

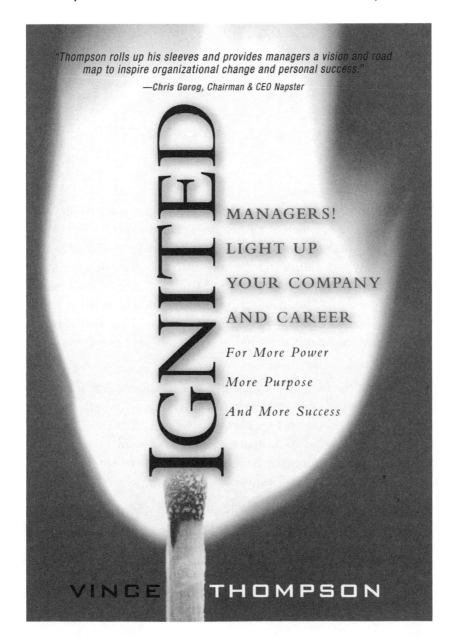

"Thompson rolls up his sleeves and provides managers a vision and road map to inspire organizational change and personal success."
—Chris Gorog, Chairman & CEO Napster

IGNITED

MANAGERS!

LIGHT UP

YOUR COMPANY

AND CAREER

For More Power

More Purpose

And More Success

VINCE THOMPSON

From the Introduction of *Ignited: Managers!*
Light Up Your Company and Career for More
Power More Purpose and More Success
(ISBN-13: 9780131492486).

ACTION WITH TRACTION

Banging Pots

The time: Almost 25 years ago. It was my second day at a new summer job, working in the kitchen of a local diner. The dish tank was hot and humid. Behind me sat a row of plastic trays filled with greasy dishes. In front, a busboy was sliding another tray onto the table, slopping dirty dishwater onto my new tennis shoes and the soggy rubber mats below. After three-and-a-half hours of scrubbing plates and glasses, my hands were sore, my shirt soaked with dishwater, and my hair matted to my forehead. I leaned against the stainless steel table for a minute to catch my breath.

With a bang of the swinging door, Rusty, our cowboy cook, came flying around the corner, a cast iron burner in each hand. "What's up, boy? I didn't hear any noise, so I thought you weren't working. Take these things and degrease 'em. And lemme give you a word of advice. You wanna take a break, you better bang some pots. You better sound busy. No noise from the dish tank means work ain't getting done... you got it?"

I had just learned one of my first lessons in business: *Look busy. Act busy. Sound busy. And if you're not accomplishing anything, at least bang some pots.*

Flash forward. I'm selling TV ad time in a cubicle at a large firm on mid-Wilshire in Los Angeles. I am one more person in a sea of blue blazers (standard apparel for assistants with aspiration). We knew it was a competition: One of us would be getting the promotion. Which one? The one who paid the dues and looked the part. The one who *looked busy.*

Of course, this conflicts with the things we're taught in training programs on time management and productivity, and with the slogans tossed around in the latest books on leadership:

"Don't work hard, work smart!"

"Collapse time!"

"Achieve balance!"

"Focus like a laser on what's essential!"

All of these ideas sound good... but how do we do it?

How do we "collapse time" when, after answering our last six voicemail messages we find that nine more have piled up in the mailbox? How do we "achieve balance" when our company is behind the eight ball and struggling to launch that quarter-saving new product ahead of schedule? What happens when there's a changing of the guard? What happens when sales are off? What do those in the executive suite want and expect?

We all know the real answer. They want to see activity. They want production reports, sales reports, and marketing reports. They want to hear phones ringing, keyboards clicking, printers buzzing. They take comfort in knowing we're doing all we can. They want to hear the sound of banging pots.

The pressure to join the potbangers is intense. It's one of the big reasons that sensible concepts like job-sharing and telecommuting have taken so long to catch on in most corporations: "I can't work at home. If the boss doesn't see me in the office, he'll think I'm not working." Being productive is less important than being *seen* to be productive. But we all know, deep inside, that the noise from our banging is ultimately meaningless. We long to trade the treadmill of endless, ineffectual *action* for the lasting value of traction.

Traction is when our efforts in the workplace make a genuine, measurable, and lasting difference... when the things we try to do *get* done and *stay* done.

From the Introduction of *Ignited: Managers! Light Up Your Company and Career for More Power More Purpose and More Success* (ISBN-13: 9780131492486).

Most managers achieve traction, but usually in the form of sporadic breakthroughs that lurch them forward, then leave them to sit, exhausted, until they can build energy, purpose, and focus once again. It's better than nothing. Our goal is to gain *real* traction, traction that cuts deeper with every move, which carves a path and carries momentum into the future.

In order to achieve this level of traction, we must create and nurture an environment for ourselves and our team members where traction is second nature. It starts with our bosses, their goals, their needs, and our alignment with them. With alignment attained, we can employ a host of tools to keep us on the path to the traction we desire.

In the pages that follow, you'll consider the concept of Management Value Added, a powerful tool for setting your course. You'll explore the difference between traction and slippage, and how to build a portfolio of projects that stick rather than slip. Building upon these concepts, you'll look at achieving group traction and offer some new ideas for ensuring follow-through.

To read more, buy *Ignited: Managers! Light Up Your Company and Career for More Power More Purpose and More Success* (ISBN-13: 9780131492486) at a bookstore or online.

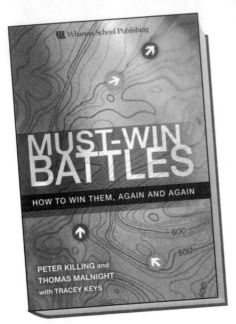

Must-Win Battles
How to Win Them, Again and Again
BY PETER KILLING, THOMAS MALNIGHT,
AND TRACEY KEYS

Must-Win Battles shows leaders exactly how to identify the 3 to 5 critical challenges most likely to make or break their businesses—and then mobilize people and resources to successfully execute on them. This book draws on the authors' exceptional experience as world-class consultants and leading-edge business researchers, and builds on the highly successful executive program they created for IMD, one of the world's best business schools. The authors show leaders how to cut through uncoordinated initiatives, create a short list of true "must-wins," focus relentlessly on them, and infuse their organizations with renewed energy and effectiveness. Along the way, discover how to recognize which victories will make the greatest difference, avoid unwinnable battles, drive consensus when somebody's ox is inevitably being gored, make sure must-win battles are specific and measurable, and change the behavior of your top management team to lock in this laser-sharp focus for future battles.

ISBN 0131990497, ISBN-13 9780131990494, © 2006, 272 pp., $27.99 USA, $34.99 CAN

Firms of Endearment
How World-Class Companies
Profit from Passion and Purpose
BY RAJENDRA SISODIA, DAVID WOLFE,
AND JAGDISH SHETH

It's a fact: People are increasingly searching for higher meaning in their lives, not just more possessions. This trend is transforming the marketplace, the workplace, and the very soul of capitalism. Increasingly, today's most successful companies are those who've brought love, joy, authenticity, empathy, and soulfulness into their businesses: companies that deliver emotional, experiential, and social value, not just profits. *Firms of Endearment* illuminates this: the most fundamental transformation in capitalism since Adam Smith. It's not a book about corporate social responsibility: it's about building companies that can sustain success in a radically new era. It's about great companies like IDEO and IKEA, Commerce Bank and Costco, Wegmans and Whole Foods: how they've earned powerful loyalty and affection from all their stakeholders, while achieving stock performance that is truly breathtaking. It's about gaining "share of heart," not just share of wallet. It's about aligning the interests of all your stakeholders, not just juggling them. It's about understanding how the "new rules of capitalism" mirror the self-actualization focus of our aging society. It's about building companies that leave the world a better place. Most of all, it's about why you must do all this, or risk being left in the dust... and how to get there from wherever you are now.

ISBN 0131873725, ISBN-13 9780131873728 © 2007, 320 pp., $27.95 USA, 34.95 CAN